W.T. GRAHAM

THE BRITISH TRAVELLING POST OFFICE

PETER JOHNSON

LONDON

IAN ALLAN LTD

First published 1985

ISBN 0 7110 1459 0

© Ian Allan Ltd 1985

Published by Ian Allan Ltd, Shepperton, Surrey;
and printed by Ian Allan Printing Ltd at their works
at Coombelands in Runnymede, England.

Contents

Introduction and acknowledgements

The reasons given for taking an interest in stamps and postal history are many and varied, like those given for taking an interest in various aspects of railways and their operations. When an interest in particular aspects of these subjects is combined the observer might well say, 'How quaint', but their proponents will be just as sincere in their beliefs, and as varied with their reasons.

The combination of railways and stamp collecting, to provide railway philately, may take many forms. Those interested in travelling post offices can pursue their interest via the vehicles used, the services operated, or the postal markings applied to the mail carried. They probably, though few would admit it, owe their allegiance to the romance engendered by trains which run, beyond the public gaze, through the dark hours of the night.

In the United Kingdom travelling post offices (TPOs) are those trains run at the behest of the Post Office, using specialised rolling stock in which mail is carried and sorted en route. Some run in passenger trains, some are exclusively for the mails, but all are worthy of observation and comment. (It is worth noting that other countries run, or have run, TPO services, but none appears to have developed a sorting network in the same way as that operated in this country. TPOs are not confined to trains, for example the Seychelles Post Office is one of several which operate a TPO aboard a ship, and the United States is notable for building up, and running down, a mobile system which had mail sorted in road, as well as rail, vehicles.)

It is probably because of their night-time excursions that travelling post offices have received more attention from philatelists than from railway enthusiasts as postmarks can be collected at convenient times. It is true that the existence of some services is only known because some collector has decided to seek out the reason behind the use of a particular datestamp.

It is because they run at night that few photographs exist of operating TPOs. The short summer nights bring the early evening departures and pre-breakfast-time arrivals within the grasp of keen photographers but they are few and far between. Most photographs of TPOs are static, either rolling stock ex-works or station scenes, and these were taken mainly for official purposes.

Although the rolling stock could be considered separately from the services, and separately from the philatelic side, it would be unwise if a proper picture is to be obtained, for each is dependent upon the other. The purpose of this volume is to bring all three together to serve as an introduction to the newcomer to the subject as a whole, and also to anyone who has previously taken an interest in one aspect or another.

Without the personnel who have operated the services since 1838 there would be no TPOs and life would be a lot less interesting for both collectors and enthusiasts; it is with pleasure that this book is dedicated to the Gentlemen of the TPOs.

Acknowledgements
I doubt if anyone could compile a volume

such as this without outside help and assistance. In this case I owe a debt of gratitude to two major sources, for without them it would not have been possible.

As it will be seen, a large amount of data contained herein was obtained from official sources and I thank the Manager of the Post Office's TPO Section for allowing me access to it. The personnel I came into contact with did everything possible to ensure that I received the best information available.

Harold Wilson has conducted a great deal of historical research into travelling post offices. Much of this has been published by the Railway Philatelic Group and I am grateful to have been able to use it. Further it was an honour to be involved in the publication of Harold's efforts a few years ago, for I know many others have also benefited from the results of his labours, both literary and philatelic.

For assistance with additional research I would like to thank the staffs of the National Railway Museum Library and the Post Office Archives; I also enjoyed using the facilities relating to the Transport History Collection in the Library of the University of Leicester. Paul Bailey, M. S. King, G. P. Roberts, Chris Whitehead and David Zeidler provided imformation and support for which I thank them.

H. C. Casserley, Michael Collins, Derek Cross, Colin Flint, R. C. Riley, F. W. Shuttleworth and P. H. Swift exerted themselves to provide suitable photographs. This was not an easy matter and it will be appreciated that some vehicles and services are more readily photographed than others. Thanks, too, to John Mackintosh for processing services.

During the years since I joined the Railway Philatelic Group many of its officers and members have become friends, always ready to help with a project or provide information; several have already been mentioned. In the context of this book, I would like to express my thanks to Mike Hunt and Tony Goodbody for providing the details needed to plan my early TPO expeditions. Tony and Roger Harrison, respectively, masterminded the mass TPO mailings of 1975 and 1980. Information regarding TPOs is regularly published in the Group's quarterly journal, *Railway Philately*. For information on Group activities send a stamped addressed envelope to the Secretary at 15 Mount Pleasant Lane, Bricket Wood, St Albans, Herts AL2 3UX.

In thanking those involved in the publication of this volume, it remains only to say that responsibility for any errors or omissions should be laid at the door of the author.

Peter Johnson
Leicester
September 1984

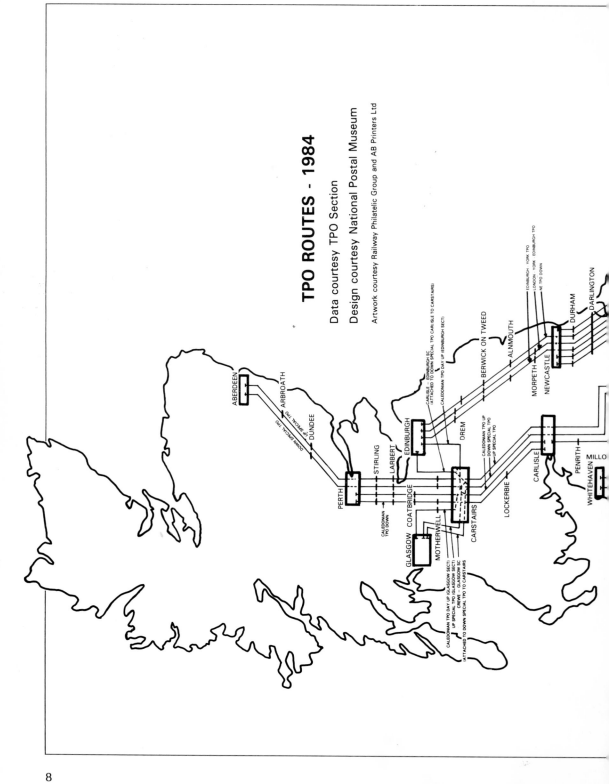

TPO ROUTES - 1984

Data courtesy TPO Section

Design courtesy National Postal Museum

Artwork courtesy Railway Philatelic Group and AB Printers Ltd

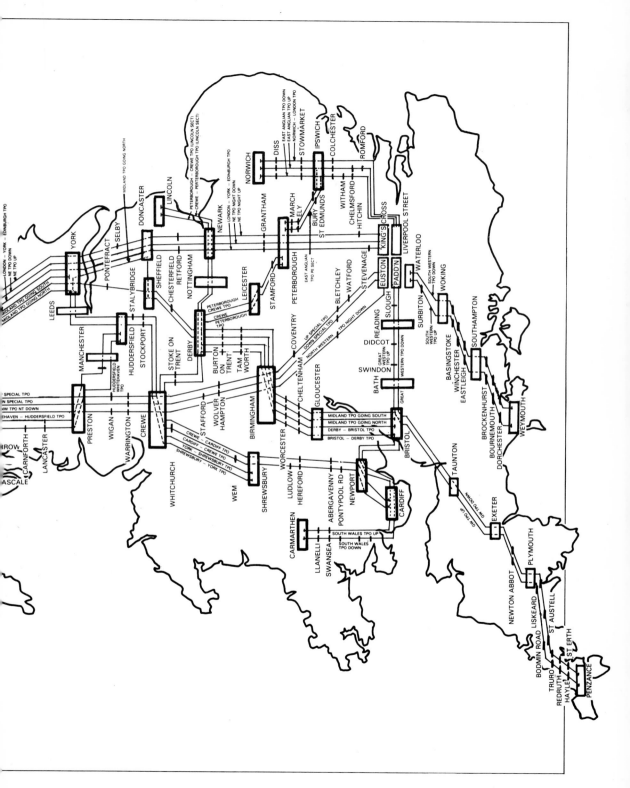

1 The Travelling Post Office

Prior to the introduction of the railways mail handling in these islands was slow and often unreliable. The Romans had introduced a postal system of considerable complexity and efficiency but it rapidly disappeared when the empire collapsed. Medieval monarchs and governments took little or no interest in the provision of private communications, often leaving it to business interests to develop their own systems. It was only with the coming of the Renaissance that governments began to take a positive interest in developing communications over and above those required for their own needs.

During the reign of Queen Elizabeth I, private persons were allowed to use the system set up for the transmission of state papers between London and Dublin. Between London and Holyhead alone, the journey took 29hr in summer and 41hr in winter before

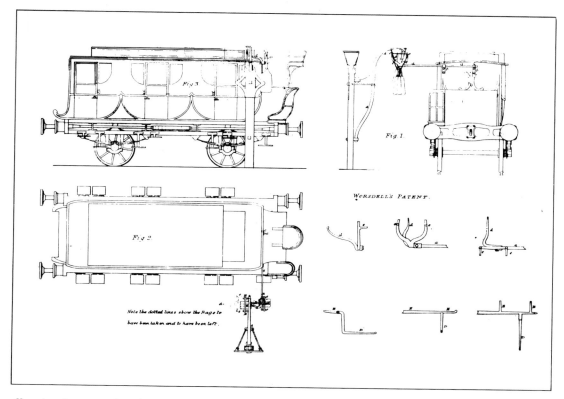

Note the dotted lines show the flaps to have been taken and to have been left.

WORSDELL'S PATENT.

allowing for stops for changing horses etc.

In 1635 a royal proclamation reorganised the inland service in an attempt to make the carriage of mails self sufficient, as the royal purse was finding the costs incurred a burden. It was decreed that the posts should cover at least 120 miles per day. Where a post existed the public was not allowed to use alternatives.

Despite this regulation it was not until 1657 that an Act of Parliament was enacted establishing the government's monopoly and the position of postmaster general. At this time mails were being carried by stage coaches at considerably less speed than the earlier scheme for state papers. For example, it took six days to travel from London to Chester. To travel by stage coach must have been an awesome experience; the roads were atrocious and the coaches often broke down because they had no springs. The rough riding of the vehicles often made passengers ill.

Improvements were not to come about until the passing of the Roads Acts, permitting the construction and operation of toll roads, in the 18th century.

Special coaches for the mails, accompanied by armed guards, commenced in 1784. These speeded up the mails considerably and London to Holyhead was reduced to 36hr and accommodation was also provided for five passengers.

The opening of the Stockton & Darlington Railway in 1825 had no influence on the carriage of mails, although it is said that letters with string tied around them were carried as parcels, to circumvent the GPO's monopoly. Its comparatively isolated situation did not put it in the position of being a forerunner in this instance.

A completely different situation arose with the opening of the Liverpool & Manchester Railway five years later. For one thing it con-

Left:
An engraving of an early TPO fitted with apparatus. *The Post Office (copyright reserved)*

Above:
The unprofitable patent. The drawings which accompanied Nathanial Worsdell's application of 1838. *P. T. Bailey Collection*

nected a large developing port with a similar industrial centre and there were parties at either end who wished to communicate and transport goods. Such were the opportunities offered that it was not long before bags of mail were being carried by rail between the two centres.

There were to be no further developments until the Grand Junction Railway opened from Birmingham to Warrington on 4 July 1837. Mails were carried from the opening but between London and Birmingham they were still carried by road. The journey time from London to Liverpool was $16\frac{1}{2}$hr. The GPO commenced negotiating with the company for terms and conditions under which the service could be expanded. Con-

sidering the company's terms too expensive it tried to obtain powers from Parliament which would apply to all railway companies. Had the GPO succeeded it would have gained complete control over the operation of the railways. Clauses in the Bill required the railways to:

Provide, at their own cost, carriages and locomotives, special, ordinary, or otherwise, to carry the mails at all hours of the day or night, at such speed, and stopping at such places and just so long as the Postmaster-General shall provide.

Replace, at their own cost, any carriages provided by them and rejected by the Postmaster-General, for any duty.

Far left:
A complete set of lineside apparatus at Penrith.
E. D. Bruton

Far below left:
**Loading apparatus on the Great Western
Railway.** *British Rail*

Left:
**With the bags in position at Harrow & Wealdstone.
Note the string which held the bags still until they
were collected, when the string broke.**
Ian Allan Library

Below left:
**The moment of impact at Berkhamsted. 25 June
1947.** *H. C. Casserley*

To inflict a penalty for disobedience of any of
its orders.

To alter or rescind any of its contracts with
the companies, by three months notice, or
without, the companies not to have similar
powers.

Obviously the companies petitioned against
the Bill for the resulting Act was more accept-
able to them. Despite this the GPO still had
wide ranging powers; it could put mails on
any train; it could ask for special trains to run
at its convenience; it could ask the companies
not to change the time of certain trains
without notifying the Post Office; and it could
ask for the provision of special rolling stock. A
similar situation still applies today.

Payments for the use of the trains commenced at £1,743 in 1838, had increased to
£490,223 in 1860 and in 1896 had reached
£1 million, an ample demonstration of the
growth of both rail and postal systems.

The proposal to sort mail on the move first
came to the fore in January 1938. It originated
with Fredrick Karstadt, a Post Office sur-
veyor, who saw a way of reducing some of
the paperwork that applied with the system
already used. It was agreed to run an experimental service, employing Karstadt's son and
another as mail clerks. The Grand Junction
Railway provided a converted horsebox for
the purpose of the experiment and the service
started at the end of January. The generally
accepted date has usually been the sixth of
that month but that has been shown to be
incorrect.

The experiment was an immediate success,
so on 28 May 1838, the railway company was

Give precedence to postal requirements, over
and above the requirements of fare-paying
passengers.
Obey the Postmaster-General's orders
respecting the conveyance, delivery, and
leaving of the mails, and the place the Post
Office carriage shall have in the train.
Further, it allowed the Post Office:
If running its own trains, to do so without
payment of any rate or tolls whatsoever.
To remove all obstructions to their locos.
To use anything, locos, carriages, ropes, etc,
of the company on every part of the line, to
work their engines for carrying the mails, and
passengers.
To repudiate any by-laws contradictory to its
powers.

asked to provide a permanent sorting carriage. This would bring the operation on the Grand Junction in line with the one recently started on the London & Birmingham Railway.

On 9 April 1838 the London & Birmingham Railway extended its Euston line from Tring to Denbigh Hall and opened its line between Rugby and Birmingham. The construction of the Kilsby Tunnel was to delay the opening of the line throughout until August. Purpose-built sorting carriages were put into service on the opened sections on 22 May. A contract authorising this, and agreeing to the carriage of mail on ordinary trains was signed a week later.

The North Union Railway was opened between Wigan and Preston on 7 November 1838. The GPO was quick to take advantage of the 225-mile length of railway thus created by amalgamating and extending the London & Birmingham and the Grand Junction railway post offices the same day.

From 20 January 1839 the day mail took six hours and needed one sorting carriage; first-class passengers were also carried. The night mail was a mixed train using a sorting carriage and a letter bag carriage and took $6\frac{1}{2}$hr. These services were the forerunners of the Down and Up Special Travelling Post Offices which operate today.

An interesting feature of mail handling at this time concerned bags destined for minor stations at which the train was not due to stop. They were thrown on to the platform as the train passed through! Even at 25mph considerable damage could be done, both to the mails and any innocent bystander! Clearly something would have to be done to improve the situation.

It was Nathanial Worsdell who designed and built the first apparatus for exchanging mail bags with a moving train. He was the Superintendent of the Grand Junction Railway's carriage works and helped his father build the *Rocket's* tender in 1829 and later his sons made names for themselves on the North Eastern Railway. Worsdell had built and tested his apparatus in 1837, before even the first sorting carriage had run, and was granted a patent for it on 4 January 1838. The GPO sought to make use of the equipment but failed to agree a price with Worsdell, who was never to profit from his invention.

The Post Office was still interested in using such a device so encouraged one of its employees, John Ramsey, to investigate the matter. Ramsey devised an apparatus which was tested successfully at Boxmoor on 30 May 1838. This was two days after the Post Office had notified Worsdell that his final offer had been refused. Despite the initial success of Ramsey's apparatus, further installations over the next two years encountered considerable difficulties. It appears that the rather complicated apparatus worked satisfactorily under test conditions, but did not stand up to normal wear and tear.

An inspector called Dicker, who was in charge of the ground installations, made many modifications and improvements, even going to the extent of building working models in his own time and at his own expense.

His efforts were rewarded on 15 April

1848 when he was able to try an apparatus of his own devising. It worked to everyone's satisfaction and was accepted for use by the Post Office. There was, however, a sting in the tail of this acceptance: it was considered possible that Dicker's apparatus might infringe Worsdell's patent — so its introduction was delayed until 1852 when the patent expired. Dicker did eventually receive £500 for his trouble and his device was to remain in use, with little modification, for over 100 years. The railway companies were paid for maintaining the ground apparatus.

The apparatus transferred mail from the ground to the TPO and vice versa. For either function to work in safety three items of equipment were required, one being common to both.

Above left:
A heavily re-touched photograph of the operation as it took place on the LNWR. *Author's Collection*

Below left:
On the train — strapping up the pouch.
Real Photos

Below:
Connecting the pouch to the traductor.
Real Photos

Below right:
Connecting the pouch to the traductor. Notice the rope for use if the traductor return mechanism failed and the bar to prevent staff from falling out. *Real Photos*

The item common to both picking up and setting down mail on the move was the pouch. These were made of stout leather and were fashioned with four flaps that could be wrapped over the contents. Leather straps passing over and around the pouch secured them. A loaded pouch could weigh anything from 20lb to 60lb. Obviously mail which was put through the exchange received quite a buffeting; from 1902, for 28 years, the Post Office had an answer for anything that looked unsuitable — an adhesive label, which read 'This Packet has been diverted from the usual route, as it appeared to be too fragile for transfer by Mail Apparatus' was affixed to appropriate items to explain any delay in delivery.

To transfer mail to a TPO the pouch was mounted on a lineside standard. The placing of these in relation to the track was critical, especially as the clearance between a loaded standard and a train was less then 18in, therefore the heads of the 10ft tall standards were turned away from the trackside when not in use. Sometimes there would be several standards at one location. The postman would attach the pouches to the standards about 10min before the train was due, usually receiving a warning gong signal from the nearest signalbox.

The pouch was removed from its standard by the carriage net, that distinctive feature of TPOs for over a century. The net had to be lowered at just the right moment if the opera-

tion was to be successful. Too soon or too late and serious damage could be done to the net (and the train) by lineside structures; the failure to effect the exchange was the least of the operator's problems. Across the mouth of the net a wire was stretched to pull the pouch off the standard; it would drop into the net and roll into the carriage. While the net was extended a warning bell sounded continuously, and a barrier was placed in the corridor connection to protect unwary staff from flying pouches.

To transfer mail to the lineside the pouch was attached to a traductor. There could be as many as four of these attached to the side of the carriage. One would be situated either side of a doorway. The operator would have to lean out of the doorway to attach the pouch, a hazardous move, for which a safety bar was provided. When extended the arm of the traductor suspended the pouch 3ft away from the carriage and about 5ft from the ground. The impact of the pouch caused the spring-loaded traductor to return inboard. If the spring failed a rope allowed the job to be done manually.

The pouch was removed from the traductor by a wire stretched across the mount of the ground net. Because it was so close to the trackside the side of the net nearest the track was collapsed down when not in use.

Other ground equipment was a warning board placed 250ft before the apparatus for the use of the TPO crew, and a black and yellow enamelled board which was illuminated at night when the apparatus was to be used. This was for the benefit of the loco crew. It was sometimes mounted on the side of a small hut which gave the waiting postman some shelter.

Another type of apparatus was described in the 25 October 1856 issue of *Mechanics' Magazine*. It was invented by A. D. Lacy, of Knayton in Yorkshire, who had obtained a patent. It appeared to use the same apparatus for both collecting and despatching, in a similar manner to that used for exchanging single-line tablets at speed. It is not known how long Mr Lacy pursued the marketing of his patent.

The original services were known as railway post offices. From the 1860s some services were called sorting tenders. The reason for the distinction is unknown but it could be that the RPOs were controlled from Post Office HQ, while the STs were controlled by the postmasters of the towns they served. The sorting tenders became known as sorting carriages from 1904 and the title certainly ceased to have any operational significance after control of all services passed to the London Postal Region in the 1930s. From 1914 the RPOs were called railway sorting carriages, this title lasting until 1928 when they became travelling post offices. Other mail services have been designated Sunday sorting tenders, district sorting carriages and bag tenders.

Sunday sorting tenders evolved as a scheme to reduce the number of staff on duty

Each year, for a period around Christmas, the TPOs suspend their sorting activities and run as bag tenders. In this guise they run with a reduced staff, handling only bagged mail. Special datestamps are issued, but for internal documentation only. Other bag tenders operate all the year round, the Preston-London and the London-Norwich being staffed and using Post Office vehicles. The Preston-London bag tender exists to relieve the Up Special TPO of Datapost traffic. This is a guaranteed next day delivery service which commenced in 1970 to deal with computer material and greatly expanded in scope subsequently.

From 1860 the public were allowed to post letters on to the TPOs on payment of an extra fee in addition to the normal postage. This was called the late fee and in 1860 it was 2d, although there were some variations in different parts of the country. In 1880 it was reduced to $\frac{1}{2}$d and remained thus until 30 June 1969 when it was increased to 1d. When the currency was decimalised on 15 February 1971 the late fee was converted to $\frac{1}{2}$p. It became 1p on 24 June 1974 and was abolished, for letters, on 27 September 1976. Letters are still accepted on the TPOs, although they must be prepaid at the first class rate and posted in the boxes provided, either on the trains or at certain stations. This service is little used, largely because of lack of publicity, but there are a few commercial undertakings who find it worthwhile. One organisation uses specially printed envelopes which draw attention to the fact that their mail was posted on a train. Apart from that the largest use of the late service is made on Budget night; a number of City finance houses vie to get their analyses of the Chancellor's intentions into the post with same day postmarks — the TPOs allow them to achieve their objective. The London termini which originate TPOs have late letter boxes, which can only be used at certain times, for mail which will be sent by TPO. Similar boxes exist

at the London Chief Office on Sundays. On Saturday nights mail from towns around London, which could not be sorted before the usual up working reached London, was put on a down duty for transferring to an up duty at a suitable distance away from the capital. Seven services started on 20 April 1850 when 23 fewer men were required at the London Chief Office the following day. Rowland Hill, whose ideas for postal reform lead to the introduction of the Universal Penny Post and the 1d black postage stamp, recorded the event in his diary. The services were eventually merged with the district sorting carriages.

Between 1857 and 1863 nine district sorting carriages were introduced. They travelled out of London picking up London-bound mail and sorted it on the up journey. They were withdrawn in 1869.

at Bournemouth, Newton Abbot and Newcastle.

Prior to decimalisation another late fee, of 1/6d, existed for registered and recorded delivery mail. It was converted to 7½p then, raised to 10p on 24 June 1974 and remains so at the time of writing.

An examination of the historical list which follows will reveal a number of changes which took place in 1885. The acceleration of the Scottish mails which took place that year had far reaching effects. The most important aspect was the introduction of the Special Mail between Euston and Aberdeen, supplementing the North Western and Caledonian TPOs. A number of other services were introduced or extended to connect with the 'Special' and the basic pattern of services which evolved on the west coast route still exists today. The 'Special' was to become the Up Special TPO and the North Western and Caledonian TPOs evolved to become the Down Special TPO. Between them they provide the most comprehensive TPO service in the country. The Up Special, for example, runs to 12 postal vehicles and conveys a Manchester-Birmingham BG from Crewe to Birmingham. On an average night 250,000 letters and packets will be sorted, many hundreds of mail bags will be carried as stowage and 1,100 items of Datapost will be dealt with.

In 1938 the TPO service celebrated its centenary and efforts were made to see that the public knew all about it. The GPO's film unit made a film, 'Night Mail', a documentary which has become a classic still demanded by audiences everywhere. With some film maker's licence, it told the story of a night on the Down Special. The poem which accompanied the film introduced the then unknown W. H. Auden to a wider audience. An exhibition was held at Euston station where TPO rolling stock through the ages was displayed. The LMS built a replica of a 1838 Grand Junction Railway TPO coach which is still to be seen at the National Railway Museum in York. A West Coast Joint Stock TPO coach of 1885 (also shown at Euston) can also be seen at York.

Also in 1938 the GPO commissioned the well known model making firm of Bassett-Lowke to build a scale working model of the Up Special. Taking three months to build, the train had three sorting carriages, a stowage, van and two brake vans. It was hauled by a 'Royal Scot' class loco, the entire train being 17ft long. The layout for the model was a circuit of 120ft. At a scale of ³⁄₈in to 1ft, the model was finely detailed, both internally and externally, even the door of the clothes locker opened to reveal a coat hook! The model was electrically driven, with the exchange apparatus working automatically as the train circuited the track, and the warning bell rang while the net was extended. The fate of the model is unknown.

Although some services were withdrawn because of staffing problems TPO operation was not greatly affected by World War 1. The same could not be said with regard to the second. All the TPOs were withdrawn by 21 September 1940, while the Up and Down Specials and the Great Western services continued to operate as bag tenders. Sorting was resumed on these services on 1 October 1945 but late fee letters were not allowed until 7 July 1947. Other TPOs were restored during the closing years of the 1940s, but 34 of the pre-war total of 77 failed to return. This cutback was caused by the reduced number of deliveries, making it possible to withdraw most of the day mails. Some additional services were introduced to complete the network, the last being in 1966. A shortage of sorters with an intimate knowledge of apparatus operations was the reason the TPO section published a number of TPO route guides at this time. These showed all the landmarks associated with the use of the apparatus and reminded or informed staff of their locations.

The Irish Mail celebrated its centenary in 1948. The Chester & Holyhead Railway had opened its line across Anglesey to Holyhead on 1 August 1848. The line from Bangor to Anglesey, including the Brittania Bridge,

Top right:
Late posting boxes — 1: On the train. *Author*

Far top right:
Late posting boxes — 2: Bournemouth. *Author*

Right:
Late posting boxes — 3: King's Cross. *Author*

Far right:
Late posting boxes — 4: Newcastle. *Author*

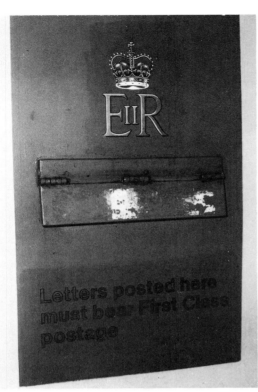

remained unfinished but it was decided to run a train from London, with mails for Dublin on the same day. The gap in the railway was covered by road transport, using Telford's suspension bridge across the Menai Straits. This was to be the regular route until the first tube of Stephenson's rail bridge was opened to traffic on 18 March 1850. A TPO was operating by 1854. The average speed from London to Holyhead was 42mph, with a loading of about 240 tons. To maintain the reliability of the services the first water troughs were laid in the track at Aber, between Bangor and Conwy in 1861. Sorting was also carried out on board the ships while crossing the Irish Sea. This finished on 10 March 1923, for the day services, and on 21 February 1925 for the night services. The TPO duties were finished during World War 2, but bagged mails continued to be carried, as is the case even now, and the equivalent down train from Euston continued to be called the 'Irish Mail' for many years afterwards.

In 1959 British Rail commenced the construction of a new fleet of TPO rolling stock to replace the pre-nationalisation vehicles then in use. During the following 18 years 145 vehicles were built, some on secondhand underframes. Nominally there are three types but the building time-span has meant that there are several variations within each category. The last pre-nationalisation vehicles were withdrawn by 1978. Several have been preserved, with two put into working order, capable of demonstrating the exchange apparatus. The owners of the others have also declared that this is their ambition for the future.

On Wednesday 7 August 1963 the Up Special TPO left Aberdeen as usual but by the time it reached London it had hit the headlines in a big way. In the early hours of Thursday morning the train was stopped at false signals between Leighton Buzzard and Cheddington by thieves who then separated the locomotive and the first two coaches from the train. After subduing the loco crew the front of the train was moved to a convenient underbridge, where the coaches were broken into and robbed of the currency they were carrying.

Slightly more than £2½ million was stolen. The currency was used bank notes being returned to the Bank of England for destruc-

Left:
Late posting boxes — 5: Newton Abbot. *Author*

Below:
Late posting boxes — 6: Waterloo. *Author*

tion, a function since removed from TPOs. The incident became known as the 'Great Train Robbery', and despite the arrest, and subsequent imprisonment of some of those involved, most of the money was never recovered. It was a black night for both British Rail and the Post Office.

In 1968 the Post Office introduced a two-tier postal system. The objective was to reduce the amount of mail posted in the afternoon and requiring next-day delivery. A higher rate was charged for first class mail, for which the customer required a next-day delivery, and a lower rate for second class items which could be sorted at slack times and delivered later. This affected the TPOs as it was decided they should only handle first class items. As the system settled down it became apparent that there was insufficient overnight business to sustain some of the services. The first to go was the Plymouth-Bristol TPO on 3 March 1972 and 1977 saw the demise of the South Eastern TPO on 18 February and the Manchester-Glasgow SC on 3 June. The Highland TPO was withdrawn on 7 October 1978 while the most recent withdrawal was the Crewe-Bangor TPO on 19 February 1979.

The use of the mail exchange apparatus began to decline after World War 2. This was partly because of the reduction in the number of postal distribution centres with the increased use of motor vehicles for local distribution. Also the improved acceleration and braking capabilities of diesel and electric locomotives made it possible to introduce new or longer station stops where necessary. The last apparatus in use was at Penrith, in Cumbria, when the last pickup was made by the Up Special TPO and the last despatch by the North Western TPO on 3 October 1971.

The Post Office offered to make available sets of apparatus to interested parties who could make use of them. To date working demonstrations have been established by the Great Western Society at Didcot, using a Great Western Railway vehicle, and by Railway Vehicle Preservations Ltd, at Quorn & Woodhouse station on the Great Central Railway, using a London & North Eastern Railway vehicle.

In 1979 the Post Office expanded its overnight airmail service, for first class and Datapost items, with a network based on Speke Airport in Merseyside and, from 1982, on East Midlands Airport in Leicestershire. The air services are designed to be complimentary to the rail services and they are integrated at some points. There are no plans, at present, for air to take over from rail, but greater integration of all types of transport will undoubtedly evolve in the future.

The opening of the Liverpool & Manchester Railway in 1830 was commemorated by a set of postage stamps issued on 12 March 1980. The five stamps showed typical L&M rolling stock, one vehicle being a mail coach. On the nights of 11 and 12 March members of the Railway Philatelic Group organised a mass TPO mailing with covers bearing the new stamps. A total of 26 trains were visited, some on both nights. British Rail ran a first day cover train from Manchester to Liverpool and back using *Flying Scotsman*. The real anniversary was celebrated on 11 November 1980, when the Post Office chartered a special train from Liverpool to York hauled by Stanier Pacific *Duchess of Hamilton*, so commemorating 150 years of carrying mail by rail.

As the service now operates, the objectives

RESTORATION OF T.P.O'S. 3RD PHASE OCT.1946.

THIS BOOKLET HAS BEEN PREPARED TO HELP THE CARRIAGE MAIL BAG APPARATUS ATTENDANT TO BECOME FAMILIAR WITH THE ROUTE OF THE T.P.O'S ON THE L.N.E.R. ROUTE BETWEEN LONDON (KINGS CROSS) AND EDINBURGH.

IT SUPPLEMENTS, BUT DOES NOT SUPERSEDE, THE APPARATUS WORKING MARKS BOOK WHICH IS RECOGNIZED AS THE OFFICIAL RECORD FOR ALL APPARATUS STATIONS.

THE INFORMATION CONTAINED HEREIN HAS BEEN SUPPLIED BY THE L.N.E. RAILWAY COMPANY, TO WHOM I AM INDEBTED FOR THEIR CO-OPERATION IN PREPARING THIS PUBLICATION.

F. G. FIELDER.
CHIEF SUPERINTENDENT.
T. P. O. SECTION.

ABBREVIATIONS & SYMBOLS

FIX ON	FITTING DROP STRAP OF POUCH TO TRADUCTOR ARM AT A GIVEN POINT PRIOR TO DESPATCH FROM APPARATUS CARRIAGE.
L	LOWERING OF CARRIAGE NET FOR RECEIPT OF MAILS.
E	EXTENDING OF POUCHES FOR DELIVERY INTO LINESIDE NET.
L & E	COMBINED OPERATION OF LOWERING CARRIAGE NET FOR RECEIPT OF MAILS & EXTENDING POUCHES FOR DELIVERY INTO WAYSIDE NET.
N	LINESIDE APPARATUS NET
1.	LINESIDE APPARATUS DESPATCHING STANDARD (FIGURE INDICATES THE NUMBER OF POUCHES WHICH CAN BE DESPATCHED)
	WHITE BOARD SHOWING POINT AT WHICH MAILS SHOULD BE DESPATCHED OR RECEIVED. (NOT PROVIDED AT ALL APPARATUS POINTS)

BRIDGE OVER LINE   TUNNEL

LINE OVER   RIVER OR CANAL

JUNCTION   VIADUCT

YORK STATION

† NOT ON SATURDAYS   †† SATURDAYS ONLY.
* NOT ON SUNDAYS   § SUNDAYS ONLY.

---

are quite clear; the down services from London are intended to provide a connection with the first delivery in England and Wales for mail posted in London and the home counties during the late afternoon. At the same time it is hoped to achieve a next-day delivery in Scotland for mail posted at the same time. The principal services to London are timed to connect with the first delivery in the London districts and many other places. Cross-country and feeder services supplement the main services and connect with them to provide a countrywide TPO service, all aimed at the first delivery. By the time a TPO arrives at its destination all the mail still on the train will have been sorted into bundles for individual post offices. In some cases, such as on the Great Western down, after Plymouth, street sorting will be carried out for Penzance, an exercise designed to save time at the receiving office.

To provide this service there are 39 TPOs

operating every weeknight with a staff of 658. Each year the 144 TPO coaches cover about 5½ million miles in the course of their duties. Approximately 310 million first class letters and packets are sorted on board every year. Millions of bags of mail also travel by TPO for part of their journey from one place to another. Many more millions of bags of mail also travel on ordinary service trains. On a typical night about 15,000 bags of Datapost items are carried by TPO for some stage of their journey. All in all, some impressive figures for a very impressive service.

Below:
A typical page from the same booklet.
Author's Collection

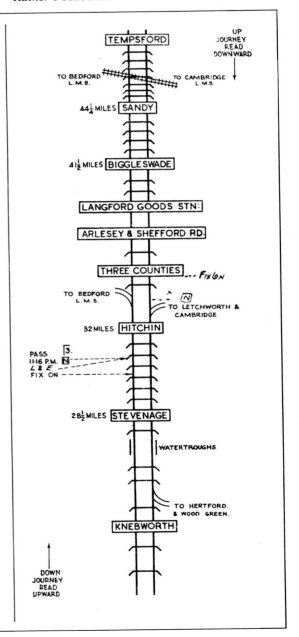

2 A Historical Survey of TPO Services

A historical list of TPO services follows. It is necessarily abbreviated, being restricted to dates of commencement and cessation or alteration. Where the route followed is not obvious from the title this is also given. The introduction or extension of many services often coincided with the opening to traffic of the relevant sections of railway. Despite this the facts of the early histories have not always been well recorded, which accounts for a certain vagueness regarding some of the original services.

Aberdeen & Elgin Sorting Carriage
Commenced 24 October 1904, ceased 3 June 1916. Previously the North of Scotland Sorting Carriage.

Bangor Railway Post Office
Ran during the 1850s from Leeds to Holyhead.

Bangor and Crewe Travelling Post Office
This service emerged when the Bangor & Leeds RPO was split into two parts in the 1870s. The datestamps were inscribed 'From East' for the Down working and 'From West' for the Up working. Renamed the Bangor-Crewe TPO on 17 February 1930. Ceased 9 February 1979. A parcel sorting carriage was conveyed between 1885 and 5 November 1915. As with the Bangor RPO, the working was actually to and from Holyhead.

Bangor & Leeds Railway Post Office
Successor to the Bangor RPO until the creation of the Bangor & Crewe TPO in the 1870s.

Bangor & Normanton Railway Post Office
Possibly the Bangor RPO extended to Normanton to connect with the Midland RPO.

Below:
The Cornwall Railway sorting carriage, with papier mâché body, on the Falmouth branch c1870.
R. J. Woodfin/H. S. Wilson Collection

Berwick & Newcastle Sorting Tender
Little is known this service, although a number of postmark impressions dated 1888 exist.

Birmingham-Bristol Travelling Post Office
Founded on 3 July 1938 when the Bristol-Gloucester TPO was extended to Birmingham. Extended to Derby on 27 March 1949.

Birmingham & Crewe Sorting Carriage
The Birmingham & Stafford ST extended, probably from 1885. Became the Birmingham-Crewe SC on 17 February 1930 and the Birmingham-Crewe TPO on 3 November 1930. Ceased 5 March 1967.

Birmingham-Liverpool Railway Post Office
The original experimental TPO which ran in a converted horse-box during 1838.

Birmingham & Stafford Sorting Tender
Commenced February 1856, replaced by Birmingham & Crewe SC in 1885.

Bridlington Sorting Carriage
Serviced by the Hull ST from 5 June 1892 this SC permitted Bridlington's first delivery to

commence 35min earlier than formerly. Extended to Leeds from 1913 and ceased on 30 October 1916. Reinstated between Bridlington and Hull only as a summer service from 17 June 1919 to 30 October 1926.

Brighton Sorting Carriage
Commenced 1 July 1859. Extended to Hastings on 1 January 1876. The London terminal was London Bridge.

Brighton & Hastings Sorting Carriage
The Hastings portion of the Brighton SC from 1 January 1876. Ceased 31 March 1916.

Bristol Sorting Carriage
Probably reserved accommodation on the Midland TPO between Derby and Bristol for pre-sorting Bristol mail before arrival. Probably ran from the turn of the century until World War 1.

Bristol-Birmingham Travelling Post Office
As for the Birmingham-Bristol TPO.

Bristol-Derby Travelling Post Office
Commenced on 27 March 1949 when the

Birmingham-Bristol TPO was extended to Derby.

Bristol & Exeter Railway Post Office
Commenced 1 December 1859. Known as the North Mail, since it connected with the Midland RPO, and to distinguish it from the Day Mail over the same route, which was a connection off a London train. Extended to Newton Abbot in July 1872. Title changed to Bristol & Exeter TPO on an unknown date.

Bristol & Exeter Travelling Post Office (Day Mail)
Commenced 1875, ceased 1917.

Bristol-Gloucester Travelling Post Office
Commenced 1 June 1910 as the Gloucester & Bristol TPO. A Bag Tender had been operated on this route from 1899. Extended to Birmingham on 3 July 1938.

Bristol-London Sorting Carriage
Commenced in the 1860s. Renamed the Bristol-London TPO on 7 July 1930. The Up was not reinstated after World War 1 until 1932. Ceased 21 September 1940.

Left:
The Bangor-Crewe TPO at Rhyl on 27 October 1977. *Larry Goddard*

Below:
The Plymouth-Bristol TPO with a GWR carriage at Whiteball. 21 July 1956. *R. C. Riley*

Bottom:
A 'County' on the Plymouth-Bristol TPO at Cowley Bridge Junction. 16 July 1958. *R. C. Riley*

Bristol & Newton Abbot Travelling Post Office
Commenced July 1872. Extended to
Plymouth in October 1895.

Bristol & Penzance Travelling Post Office
The Bristol-Plymouth TPO extended to
Penzance on 11 February 1896. Cut back to
Plymouth because of the war on 14 August
1916 and renamed accordingly on 14 April
1930.

Bristol-Plymouth Travelling Post Office
Created by extending the Bristol & Newton
Abbot TPO to Plymouth in October 1895.
Extended to Penzance on 11 February 1896.
Cut back to Plymouth in 1916, reverting to
the Bristol-Plymouth title on 14 April 1930.
Ceased on 3 March 1972.

*Bristol, Shrewsbury & Normanton Travelling
Post Office*
Created on 15 October 1895 when the
Shrewsbury & Normanton TPO was extended
to Bristol. Extended to York on 1 July 1902
becoming the Bristol, Shrewsbury & York
TPO.

*Bristol, Shrewsbury & York Travelling Post
Office*
Commenced 1 July 1902 as described above.
Became the Cardiff-York TPO in June 1910.

Caledonian Railway Post Office
A Night Mail commenced operating between
Carlisle and Glasgow 10 March 1848. Later
that year extended to Perth, avoiding
Glasgow. A Day Mail started in 1848 was

extended to Aberdeen in 1849, the Night Mail
following suit in 1850, although it was 1871
before sorting was carried out after Perth. On
1 February 1859 the Night Down became a
Limited Mail, ie the Post Office permitted a
limited amount of passenger accommodation
to be included in the train formation. From
January 1870 the services became the
Caledonian TPO, with distinguishing
datestamps for the day and night operations.
An exclusive 'special' mail between Euston
and Aberdeen was introduced on 1 July
1885; four passenger coaches were permitted
from Perth. The stock used on the Up Limited
and the Up Special was returned North on the
Night Down, which became known as the
Down Special. The Night Up ceased in 1917
and its business transferred to the Up Special
which became the Up Special TPO. On
1 September 1923 the Night Down
amalgamated with the North Western Night
Down to become the Down Special TPO. After
a number of minor revisions the Day mails
were terminated at Perth and Carlisle in
1924. An Edinburgh portion started to serve
the Day Up, also in 1924. A Glasgow portion
followed in 1935. Both were attached to the
main train at Carstairs.

Cambridge District Sorting Carriage
Started as a sorting tender in 1850, the DSC
superseding it in 1863. Ceased in 1869. Mails

Below:
**The Midland TPO going north near Yate,
Gloucestershire, in July 1955.** *G. F. Heiron*

from London surburbs were collected on the Down run for sorting on Up trains.

Cardiff-Crewe Railway Sorting Carriage
Created when the Cardiff-York TPO operation was split into two on 4 October 1920. Became an SC in 1929 and a TPO on 14 April 1930.

Cardiff & York Travelling Post Office
In June 1910 the Bristol, Shrewsbury and York TPO was extended to Cardiff. On 4 October 1920 the working was divided to give the Cardiff-Crewe RSC, already mentioned, and the Shrewsbury-York RSC.

Carlisle & Ayr Sorting Tender
Commenced 23 November 1874 and became an SC in 1904. On 1 October 1921 became the Carlisle-Ayr RSC, a title which lasted until 6 November 1929 when it became the Carlisle-Ayr SC. Ceased 9 November 1969.

Carlisle & Edinburgh Sorting Tender
Commenced experimentally in September 1858 and made permanent in 1860. Withdrawn between 1 December 1877 and May 1885 when the duty was replaced by a Carstairs-Edinburgh working. In January 1922 the Up working became the Edinburgh Section of the Up Special. The Down became the Carlisle-Edinburgh SC in October 1924.

Camarthen & Newcastle Emlyn Sorting Carriage
The Llandyssul Sorting Tender, a Carmarthen-Llandyssul duty, extended to Newcastle Emlyn in July 1895. Ceased 1 May 1904.

Carnforth & Whitehaven Travelling Post Office
The Whitehaven ST, introduced in 1875, used a datestamp with the title between 1891 and 1911; its duties don't appear to have changed as a result although the service was designated a sorting carriage in 1904.

Chester & Crewe Parcel Travelling Post Office
Commenced July 1885 attached to the Bangor-Crewe TPO, extended to Bangor September 1885.

Chester & Holyhead Railway Post Office
Commenced 1854, extended to London (Euston) 1860.

Continental Night Mail
Commenced 1 September 1867, between Dover and London (Cannon Street). A Down service was introduced in 1879. Ceased 1915 but re-introduced as the London-Dover RSC in 1922.

Cornwall Sorting Tender
Commencement probably followed shortly after the Cornwall Railway opened its line from Plymouth to Truro in 1859. The duty connected with the London & Exeter TPO, the night mail, and the Bristol & Exeter, the north mail. The former ceased in 1895, on the creation of the Great Western TPO, and the latter in 1896 on the creation of the Bristol & Penzance TPO.

Crewe-Bangor Travelling Post Office
As for the Bangor & Crewe TPO.

Crewe-Birmingham Sorting Carriage
As for the Birmingham-Crewe SC.

Crewe-Cardiff Railway Sorting Carriage
Created by the division of the Cardiff & York TPO into two parts in 1920. Re-designated a sorting carriage on 6 November 1929 and became a TPO 25 June 1934.

Crewe to Liverpool Sorting Carriage
Commenced 1 July 1885, ceased 23 September 1939.

Crewe & Manchester Sorting Carriage
The Manchester Sorting Tender apparently renamed in 1908. Re-designated the Crewe-Manchester RSC from October 1915. An additional Down working was established at the same time. Ceased 23 September 1939.

Crewe-Peterborough Travelling Post Office
Commenced 6 June 1966 with a Lincoln Section which runs to and from Crewe, joining/leaving the main train at Derby. The most recent TPO to be introduced.

Dartmoor Railway Sorting Tender
Little is known of this service which may have operated in conjunction with Army manoeuvres in 1873.

Derby-Bristol Travelling Post Office
As for the Bristol-Derby TPO.

Derby & St Pancras Sorting Tender
Commenced 1877. Renamed the London &
Derby SC on 13 July 1908.

Dingwall-Perth Railway Sorting Carriage
Created when a number of changes were
made to the workings of the Highland SC in
November 1917. The Up trip had been the
Day mail, the Down the Night. Extended to
Helmsdale 6 August 1923.

Doncaster-London Travelling Post Office
The truncated Leeds-London TPO, created
7 March 1932. Ceased 21 September 1940.

Dover-London Railway Sorting Carriage
The Continental Night Mail renamed when re-
introduced 4 September 1922. The London
terminal was Holborn Viaduct except on
Sundays when it was Victoria. Ceased
5 October 1923.

Down Special Travelling Post Office
Created on 1 September 1923 by the
amalgamation of the Night North Western
and Caledonian TPOs, giving a through
working from Euston to Aberdeen.

East Anglian Travelling Post Office
Created when the Norwich ST, which ran
from Liverpool Street via Cambridge and Ely,
was modified to run via Ipswich on 3 March
1929. The King's Lynn Section ran from
Haughley Junction; on 30 October 1949 it
was extended to Peterborough. Ipswich has
been the junction for the Peterborough
portion since 1966.

Edinburgh & Berwick Sorting Tender
Little is known of this service which probably
ran in conjunction with the Edinburgh &
Newcastle ST in the latter half of the last
century.

Edinburgh & Carlisle Sorting Tender
As for the Carlisle & Edinburgh ST.

Edinburgh & Carstairs Sorting Tender
Commenced 1 December 1877. Down
working ceased 1 July 1885. Up working
ceased before World War 1.

Edinburgh & Glasgow Sorting Tender
Operated for a brief period circa 1870.

Edinburgh & Newcastle Sorting Tender
Day and Night Mails commenced in the
1870s. The duties of the Day Mail were
absorbed by the North Eastern Day TPO
when that working was extended to
Edinburgh on 30 September 1908. The Up
Night ceased on 22 May 1916. The
establishment of the London-York-Edinburgh
RSC coincided with the cessation of the Down
Night duty.

Edinburgh-York Sorting Carriage
The Up North Eastern TPO Day Mail was
reduced to operating between Edinburgh and
York on 17 October 1917. The duty was
named the Edinburgh-York SC on 18 January
1926. It became a TPO on 14 April
1930.

Exeter & Torrington Sorting Carriage
Commenced 12 August 1906. Ceased 5 May
1917.

Fife Sorting Tender
Commenced operating between Burntisland
and Tayport 1884. Extended to Dundee in
1887 and Edinburgh in 1890. The Day Mail
ceased on 6 November 1915, the Night Mail
following on 14 October 1917.

Galloway Sorting Tender
Commenced operating between Dumfries and
Stranraer on 1 May 1871. Extended to
Carlisle 1 July 1885. Designated a TPO on
14 July 1930. Ceased 1940.

Glasgow Sorting Tender
Operating between Glasgow and Carlisle, this
service commenced experimentally in
September 1858 and was made permanent in
March 1860. Known as the Glasgow &
Carlisle SC from circa 1904.

Glasgow & Carlisle Sorting Carriage
As the Glasgow ST. Extended to Preston in
1914 and named the Glasgow-Preston RSC.
Up services operated with the Up Special and
the Up Limited until 1 February 1917 when
these services amalgamated. Two Down
services restricted to Glasgow and Carlisle
operated as the Carlisle-Glasgow RSC until
February 1922 when they amalgamated and
were extended to Preston, becoming the
Preston-Glasgow RSC.

Glasgow-Preston Railway Sorting Carriage
As the Glasgow & Carlisle SC. Extended to Crewe on 15 December 1926 becoming the Crewe-Glasgow RSC, working with the Down Special from Crewe to Carstairs. Designated a sorting carriage from 6 November 1929.

Gloucester & Bristol TPO
Commenced 1 June 1910. Extended to Birmingham 3 July 1938.

Gloucester & Tamworth Railway Post Office
Commenced 1 November 1850. Became part of the Midland RPO, which operated between Gloucester and Newcastle, before 1855.

Grand Northern Railway Post Office
Commenced 22 May 1838, between Euston and Denbigh Hall, where the London & Birmingham Railway then terminated, as the London & Birmingham RPO. Extended to Preston 7 November 1838 and renamed. Lancaster was served from June 1840. Reverted to a Preston terminal February 1841 but extended to Lancaster again on 15 August 1844. Became the North Western RPO 1847.

Great Northern Travelling Post Office
Commenced 24 January 1910 between King's Cross and Newcastle. Amalgamated with the Newcastle & Edinburgh SC to form the London-York-Edinburgh RSC on 10 July 1922.

Great Northern Sorting Tender
This was a Day Mail which started operating between King's Cross and York on 1 March 1875. Became a sorting carriage in 1902.

Replaced by the London-Leeds RSC 10 July 1922.

Great Northern Travelling Post Office (Midday Mail)
A King's Cross-Doncaster working which commenced on 1 May 1885. Extended to York 28 February 1903. Ceased 6 November 1915.

Great Western District Sorting Tender
Commenced as a replacement for the Great Western Sunday ST, November 1859, operating between Paddington and Exeter. Ceased 1869.

Great Western Travelling Post Office
Created by the amalgamation of the London & Exeter RPO and the Cornwall ST in 1896. Extended to Penzance 1 January 1902.

Great Western Sunday Sorting Tender
Commenced operating between Paddington and Swindon 12 April 1850. Replaced by the Great Western DST 1859.

Greenock Sorting Tender
Commenced March 1866, operating between Glasgow and Greenock. Ceased late 1870s.

Grimsby & Lincoln Sorting Carriage
Commenced 1850s. Ceased 8 November 1915.

Grimsby & Peterborough Sorting Carriage
Commenced 1 April 1900. Ceased 30 March 1917.

Halifax Sorting Tender
Operated for a short time after 1871.

Hastings & Brighton Sorting Carriage
As for the Brighton & Hastings SC.

Helmsdale-Dingwall Railway Sorting Carriage
Commenced 6 August 1923. Became the Highland TPO (Northern Section) from 2 July 1930.

Highland Sorting Carriage
Commenced between Inverness and Aviemore June 1864. Extended to Perth July 1870. By 1876 the Night Mail had been extended to Bonar Bridge and the Day Mail to Novar. In 1876 the Night Mail was extended to Golspie and the Day Mail to Bonar Bridge. The Night Mail was extended again, to Helmsdale, in the 1880s and the Day Mail was restricted to operating between Inverness and Bonar Bridge. A number of changes took place in 1917, resulting in the Night Up and Day Down services ceasing. The Day Up and the Night Down became known as the Dingwall-Perth RSC.

Highland Travelling Post Office
In July 1930 the Perth-Helmsdale RSC and the Helmsdale-Dingwall RSC became the Highland TPO (Southern Section) and the Highland TPO (Northern Section) respectively. The Northern Section was withdrawn after 4 November 1967 and the Southern Section became simply the Highland TPO. It was withdrawn on 7 October 1978.

Holyhead-London Travelling Post Office
Day and Night mails commenced on 1 October 1860. The Day Mail ceased on 30 September 1939, the Night on 31 August 1940. This was the famous Irish Mail.

Huddersfield-Whitehaven Travelling Post Office
The Whitehaven-Stalybridge TPO extended to Huddersfield on 2 January 1966.

Hull Sorting Tender
Commenced 2 December 1867 between Hull and Milford Junction. Extended to Normanton 22 April 1869. Extended to Leeds 1903. Designated an SC from 1904. Became the Hull-Leeds SC from 29 September 1914. Ceased 30 September 1917.

Ipswich District Sorting Carriage
Commenced 14 July 1858 between Ipswich and Shoreditch. Ceased 1869.

Ipswich Sorting Tender
Commenced 1872. Became the London-Ipswich TPO on 3 March 1929.

Ipswich Sunday Sorting Tender
Commenced 20 April 1850. Absorbed by the Ipswich DSC.

Ipswich-London Travelling Post Office
The Ipswich ST renamed from 3 March 1929. Extended to Norwich 3 May 1931.

Leeds-Hull Sorting Carriage
As for the Hull ST.

Leeds & London Sorting Tender
On 4 March 1901 the London & Doncaster ST was extended to Leeds and renamed. The Down duty ceased from 6 November 1915. The Up became the Leeds-London RSC Up on 10 July 1922. (The Great Northern SC became the Down at the same time.) Designated a

Left:
The Highland TPO (Southern Section) leaving Nairn for Perth, via Forres, on Sunday 23 July 1961. *J. S. Whiteley*

TPO on 17 February 1930. Reverted to being a Doncaster-London working and named accordingly from 7 March 1932.

Lincoln-Tamworth Sorting Carriage
Known as the Lincoln ST this service commenced on 20 May 1867. It was entitled the Lincoln-Tamworth SC from 30 September 1919. Ceased 21 September 1940.

Lincoln Sorting Tender
As for the Lincoln-Tamworth SC.

Liverpool & Huddersfield Railway Sorting Carriage
Commenced 1 July 1899. Became a TPO from 14 April 1930. Ceased 1 January 1965.

Liverpool & London Travelling Post Office
Commenced 1860s. Ceased 1918.

Llandyssul Sorting Tender
This service commenced between Llandyssul and Carmarthen on 14 December 1875. Extended to Newcastle Emlyn in July 1895.

London & Brighton Sorting Carriage
Commenced 1 July 1859. Extended to become the London & Hastings SC from 1 January 1876. A London & Brighton Day Mail was established in the 1880s. From 1 December 1895 the Hastings service was reorganised, being divided into the London & Brighton SC and the Brighton & Hastings SC, these being night mails. The Down Night and Up Day Brighton duties ceased 5 March 1910. The Up Night and Down Day followed on 31 March 1916.

London-Bristol Sorting Carriage
As for the Bristol-London SC.

London & Crewe Sorting Carriage
The London & Stafford SC extended to Crewe from 1 May 1876. Ceased 30 March 1918.

London & Derby Sorting Carriage
Commenced 13 July 1908 when the Derby & St Pancras ST was renamed. Ceased 27 September 1918.

London & Doncaster Sorting Tender
Commenced 1 March 1891. Extended to Leeds 4 March 1901.

London & Dover Sorting Carriage (Continental Night Mail)
As for the Continental Night Mail.

London & Dover Sorting Carriage (French Day Mail)
Commenced 30 April 1860. Ceased during World War 1.

London & Dover Sorting Carriage (Ostend Day Mail)
Commenced 1 August 1862. Date of withdrawal not known.

London-Dover Railway Sorting Carriage
The Continental Night Mail resumed on 4 September 1922 with this title. Ceased 5 October 1923 and replaced by the London & Newhaven RSC.

London & Exeter Railway Post Office
Commenced 1 February 1855. Amalgamated with the Cornwall ST to become the Great Western TPO on 26 November 1895.

London & Folkestone Sorting Carriage
The rerouted and renamed London & Queenborough SC after 1 May 1911. Ceased 1915.

London & Holyhead Travelling Post Office
As for the Holyhead & London TPO.

London & Holyhead Travelling Post Office (Canadian Mail)
Commenced 1 September 1895. Ceased before 1908.

London & Holyhead Travelling Post Office (USA Mail)
Commenced 6 April 1895. Ceased November 1914.

London-Ipswich Travelling Post Office
As for the Ipswich-London TPO.

London & Leeds Railway Sorting Carriage
As for the Leeds & London RSC.

London-Newhaven Railway Sorting Carriage
Created when the Southern Railway decided to concentrate its Continental services on Newhaven, 7 October 1923. Became an SC in July 1929. Ceased 4 September 1939.

London-Norwich Travelling Post Office
Created on 3 May 1931 when the Ipswich-London TPO was extended to Norwich. The Down Mail ceased on 9 September 1939 for the War, and was replaced by a Bag Tender in 1948.

London & Queenborough Sorting Tender
Commenced January 1891. Ceased 1 May 1911 when the service was diverted to Folkestone.

London-York-Edinburgh Railway Sorting Carriage
Created 10 July 1922 by combining the Great Northern TPO with the Newcastle & Edinburgh SC. Designated a TPO 17 February 1930.

Manchester Sorting Tender
Commenced 14 March 1864 between Manchester and Crewe. Renamed Manchester & Crewe SC circa 1908. Became the Manchester-Crewe RSC from October 1915. Two services operated from Crewe to Manchester from this time. Withdrawn for the War 29 October 1916. The service was reintroduced by 1922 when it was known as the Manchester-Crewe SC. Ceased 23 September 1939.

Manchester-Glasgow Sorting Carriage
Commenced 10 September 1951. Ceased 3 June 1977.

Midland District Sorting Tender
Commenced, between Euston and Normanton, via Rugby, Leicester and Derby, 22 February 1859. Ceased 14 June 1869. The Up service was via the GN route.

Midland Railway Post Office Day
Commenced, between Rugby and Newcastle, 1 June 1862 when the Leeds & Rugby RPO and the York & Newcastle RPO combined. Ceased February 1873 when the York & Newcastle was reinstated.

Midland Travelling Post Office
Commenced 1855 by the union of the Gloucester & Tamworth and the Rugby & Newcastle Night Mail services. The new service was extended to Bristol at the same time. The datestamps of this service show the Up and Down duties as 'going south' and 'going north'; 'going' is often abbreviated 'G.G.'.

Newcastle-on-Tyne Sorting Tender
Commenced March 1876 between York and Newcastle but later extended to Normanton. Operated in conjunction with the Midland TPO. Ceased during World War 1.

Newcastle-London Railway Sorting Carriage
The Great Northern TPO duty after the creation of the London-York-Edinburgh TPO on 10 July 1922. Renamed the North Eastern TPO Night Up on 18 January 1926.

Newhaven-London Railway Sorting Carriage
As for the London-Newhaven RSC.

Normanton & Stalybridge Travelling Post Office
Created when the Leeds & Bangor RPO was divided into two in the 1870s. Combined with the Shrewsbury & Crewe ST 31 January 1893.

North Eastern Travelling Post Office (Day Mail)
Created 2 July 1895 when the York & Newcastle TPO was extended to Normanton and renamed. Absorbed the Edinburgh & Newcastle SC, another Day Mail, on 1 October 1908. The Down duty ceased 29 July 1916 and the Up ceased to run south of York after 17 October 1921. It became the Edinburgh-York SC from 18 January 1926.

North Eastern Travelling Post Office (Night Down)
Commenced 18 January 1926 between King's Cross and Edinburgh.

North Eastern Travelling Post Office (Night Up)
From 18 January 1926 the Newcastle-London RSC was renamed thus.

North of Scotland Sorting Carriage
Commenced 1 January 1886 replacing an un-named service which had been operating between Aberdeen and Keith. Extended to Elgin in May 1886 but cut back to Buckie in July 1889. Became the Aberdeen & Elgin SC on 21 November 1904 although it had been operating to Elgin since 1899.

Above:
The empty stock from the North Western TPO en route from Carlisle to Glasgow. Polquhap Summit, 3 April 1964. *Derek Cross*

North Western District Sorting Carriage
Commenced between Euston and Crewe
5 May 1857. Extended to Preston 31 January
1859. Ceased 21 July 1869.

North Western Sunday Sorting Tender
Operated between Euston and Crewe in the
1850s/60s.

*North Western Travelling Post Office
(Day Mail)*
The Grand Northern RPO renamed in 1847
when operating between Euston and Perth.
By 1859 it was only running to Carlisle and
by 1881 the Up trip was terminating at
Wigan, although it was extended to Crewe
during that year. By 1915 the Up duty had
been diverted to Liverpool. Ceased before
1922.

*North Western Travelling Post Office
(Mid-day Mail)*
Commenced between Euston and Crewe
1 March 1883. Ceased 6 November 1915.

*North Western Travelling Post Office
(10 pm Mail)*
Commenced 1 July 1885 between Euston and
Carlisle. From 12 July 1926 it was renamed
the North Western TPO Night Down.

*North Western Travelling Post Office Night
Down*
Commenced 8 May 1847 between Euston and
Carlisle. North of Carlisle it ran with the
Caledonian RPO. After 31 August 1923
became part of the Down Special when it was
amalgamated with the Caledonian TPO (Night
Mail). From 12 July 1926 the name was given
to the 10pm Mail.

North Western Travelling Post Office Night Up
Commenced 8 May 1847 between Carlisle
and Euston. The Caledonian RPO provided
the connection for Aberdeen mail. From
1 July 1885 there were two Up services, the
Limited and the Postal. The Limited ceased on
31 January 1917. The Postal was being called
the Up Special Mail during the 1880s but it
was not until after World War 1 that it
became the Up Special TPO.

Norwich-London Travelling Post Office
As for the London-Norwich TPO.

Norwich Sorting Tender
Commenced as a Norwich-Ely service on
2 August 1869. Extended to London, via
Cambridge, by 1893. Rerouted via Ipswich in
March 1929 and became the East Anglian
TPO.

Perth & Aberdeen Sorting Carriage
Commenced 1871. Ceased by 1893.

Perth-Dingwall Railway Sorting Carriage
As for the Dingwall-Perth RSC.

Perth-Helmsdale Railway Sorting Carriage
As for the Helmsdale-Perth RSC.

Peterborough District Sorting Carriage
Commenced between Peterborough and
London, via Ely, on 15 September 1858.
Became a TPO in 1867, performing the same
work. Superseded by the Peterborough ST
2 August 1869.

Peterborough Sorting Tender
Commenced 2 August 1869 by taking over the
duties of the Peterborough RPO. Ceased
3 June 1916.

Peterborough-Crewe Travelling Post Office
As for the Crewe-Peterborough TPO.

*Plymouth & Bristol Travelling Post Office
(Foreign Mails)*
Commenced August 1869. Probably ceased in
the 1920s.

Plymouth-Bristol Travelling Post Office
As for the Bristol-Plymouth TPO.

Portsmouth Sorting Carriage
Operated between Southampton and
Portsmouth from 1 August 1865. Ceased
6 October 1923.

Preston-Whitehaven Travelling Post Office
The Whitehaven & Carnforth ST extended to
Preston from 26 July 1926. Extended to
Stalybridge from 3 January 1965.

Preston-Glasgow Railway Sorting Carriage
As for the Glasgow-Preston RSC.

Rugby & Birmingham Sorting Carriage
Commenced January 1860. Date of
withdrawal unknown.

Rugby & Leeds Railway Post Office
Commenced October 1852. United with the
York & Newcastle RPO to form the Midland
Day RPO from 1 June 1862.

Rugby & Newcastle Railway Post Office
Commenced 1845. Routed to Tamworth and
amalgamated with the Gloucester &

Tamworth RPO to form the Midland RPO
from 1852.

St Pancras & Derby Sorting Tender
As for the Derby and St Pancras ST.

Scarborough & Whitby Sorting Carriage
These two places were possibly served by a
duty from York during the 1860s.

Shrewsbury & Aberystwyth Sorting Carriage
Commenced 1883. Became the Aberystwyth-
Shrewsbury SC from 8 September 1930.
Ceased 22 September 1939.

Shrewsbury & Crewe Sorting Carriage
Commenced 1 April 1891. Combined with the
Normanton & Stalybridge TPO to form the
Shrewsbury & Normanton TPO from
1 January 1893.

Shrewsbury & Hereford Sorting Carriage
Commenced 1 March 1885. Amalgamated
with the Shrewsbury & Tamworth SC from
28 February 1902.

Shrewsbury & Tamworth Railway Post Office
Commenced January 1857. Known as a TPO
from circa 1868 and as an SC from circa
1883. Joined with the Shrewsbury &
Hereford SC and became the Tamworth &
Hereford SC from 1 March 1902.

Shrewsbury-Tamworth Sorting Carriage
Commenced 6 July 1914. Ceased 28 February
1917.

Shrewsbury-York Railway Sorting Carriage
Created 4 October 1920 by the division of the
York-Cardiff to give this duty and the Crewe-
Cardiff SC. Became a TPO on 14 April 1930.

South Eastern Travelling Post Office
Commenced as the South Eastern RPO on
1 May 1860. The service operated between
London Bridge and Dover until 1866 when it
was diverted to Cannon Street. Known as a
TPO from 1870. The London terminal
reverted to London Bridge in 1968 but was
transferred to Victoria shortly afterwards.
Ceased 18 February 1977.

South Wales Sorting Carriage (North Mail)
Commenced 1 March 1884. Operated

between Gloucester and New Milford as a feeder and distributor of the Midland RPO. Ceased 27 October 1923.

South Wales Travelling Post Office
Commenced 3 March 1869. As with the South Wales North Mail the route was between Gloucester and New Milford. Became an ST in 1873. By 1924 Carmarthen was the western terminus; on 13 July 1925 the service was diverted to Bristol. Known as a TPO again from the turn of the century. Between 1946 and 1969 the TPO only operated as far as Milford Haven but the service reverted to Carmarthen from February 1969.

South Western District Sorting Carriage
Commenced, between Waterloo and Southampton, April 1860. Ceased 14 June 1869.

South Western Sunday Sorting Tender
Commenced 20 April 1850. Ceased June 1863.

South Western Travelling Post Office (Night)
Commenced, between Waterloo and Southampton, 19 August 1862 as an RPO. Extended to Dorchester in 1876. Bournemouth was served by a branch working from 1 October 1910. From 1 July

1915 the whole train was routed via Bournemouth. The service was extended to Weymouth from 27 November 1961.

South Western Travelling Post Office (Day)
Commenced 1866. Extended to Dorchester 30 June 1890. Operated via Bournemouth after June 1901. From 26 November 1923 the service was cut back to Bournemouth. Ceased September 1940.

Stafford & Liverpool Sorting Carriage
Commenced 18 April 1865. Ceased circa 1880s.

Stalybridge-Whitehaven Travelling Post Office
The Preston-Whitehaven TPO extended to Stalybridge from 3 January 1965. Extended to Huddersfield from 2 January 1966.

Tamworth & Hereford Sorting Carriage
The Shrewsbury & Hereford SC and the Tamworth & Shrewsbury SC amalgamated from 25 February 1902. Ceased 1914 when the Hereford-Shrewsbury portion was discontinued, the remainder becoming the Shrewsbury-Tamworth RSC.

Tamworth-Lincoln Sorting Carriage
As for the Lincoln-Tamworth SC.

Tamworth & Shrewsbury Sorting Carriage
As for the Shrewsbury & Tamworth SC.

Truro & Falmouth Sorting Tender
Commenced June 1864. Ceased 1916.

Below:
Clerestory postal stock on the Great Western Railway. *Author's Collection*

Up Special Mail Travelling Post Office
The renamed Up Postal working of the North Western TPO. The name is first known used in 1886.

Up Special Travelling Post Office
The Special Mail and Postal duties of the North Western TPO were amalgamated in 1917 to give the Up Special TPO.

Up Special Travelling Post Office Glasgow Section
The Glasgow Section of the North Western TPO Special Mail probably ran throughout its life; the portion continued after the creation of the Up Special TPO, in 1917, but was not named the Glasgow Section of the Up Special TPO until 1922.

Up Special Travelling Post Office Edinburgh Section
With the establishment of the Up Special TPO in 1922 the Up duty of the Carlisle-Edinburgh SC became the Up Special TPO Edinburgh Section. It ran as a bag tender from 1924. From 1 October 1945 until 7 October 1946 it ran as a TPO again, substituting for the Edinburgh Section of the Caledonian TPO which was not restored from its wartime break until the latter date. The trip is now known as the Edinburgh-Carstairs Bag Duty. In the 1950s parcels vans were substituted for the TPO stock used formerly. Although no mail is sorted the staff carry a datestamp for administrative purposes and late mail has been accepted and postmarked.

West Cornwall Tender
Commenced 1 March 1884 operating between Penzance and Truro. Ceased 1892.

Whitehaven Sorting Tender
Commenced between Whitehaven and Carnforth in 1875. Extended to Preston 26 July 1926.

Whitehaven & Carnforth Sorting Carriage
As for the Carnforth & Whitehaven SC.

Whitehaven-Huddersfield Travelling Post Office
As for the Huddersfield-Whitehaven TPO.

Whitehaven-Preston Travelling Post Office
As for the Preston-Whitehaven TPO.

Whitehaven-Stalybridge Travelling Post Office
As for the Stalybridge-Whitehaven TPO.

York & Newcastle Travelling Post Office
Commenced as an RPO 1 July 1853. Incorporated into the Midland RPO Day 1 June 1862. Re-established as a TPO February 1873. Extended to Normanton 1895 and became the North Eastern TPO (Day Mail).

York & Scarborough Sorting Carriage
Commenced 1 July 1899. Ceased 1928.

York-Shrewsbury Railway Sorting Carriage
As for the Shrewsbury-York RSC.

Below:
Postal stock en route from Edinburgh to Carlisle following a disruption to the normal routine. The location is Falahill, on the Waverley Route. 29 August 1956. *Ian S. Pearsall*

3 TPO Rolling Stock

The story of TPO coaching stock begins with the converted horse box used on the Grand Junction Railway for the experimental service of 1838. The carriage was provided by the railway company at the behest of the Post Office and established a precedent which still applies today, so that the fleet of vehicles applied exclusively to postal use is owned and maintained by British Rail. Throughout the years since 1838 the constructional techniques used on postal stock have usually reflected those used by the railway companies on their passenger vehicles.

Below:
The first of the British Rail sorting carriages was turned out from Wolverton in 1959. No 80300 was originally allocated to the Great Western TPO.
British Rail

Bottom:
Three of the new carriages seen at Penzance on 3 April 1960. From the left there is a brake stowage van, a stowage van (with apparatus on the far side), and an apparatus fitted sorting tender.
R. C. Riley

Above left:
No 80306 was a sorting van with no provision for apparatus. Penzance, 9 April 1964. *R. C. Riley*

Left:
This view of the sorting frame side of No 80305 shows the folding connecting doors. The branding on the left-hand end indicates that it is vacuum braked. Norwich, 5 June 1982. *Michael J. Collins*

Below left:
The stock of the York-Shrewsbury TPO being shunted at York, showing the sorting frame sides of the two sorting carriages. These vehicles were given provision for apparatus. 9 September 1963. *R. H. Short*

Above:
TPO vehicles at Carlisle on 24 March 1984. From the left, Nos 80330, 80332 and 80328 were fitted with apparatus when they were turned out from York in 1969. On the right, stowage van No 80406 was converted from a BSK in the 1960s. *Author*

Below:
The sorting frame side of No 80328. Carlisle, 3 March 1984. *Author*

For postal purposes there were, and are, obviously some differences. The sorting frames, minimal glazing, and wider sliding doors are noticeably traditional to the TPO. Until recently special liveries were also applied, although to most members of the public, the most outstanding feature was the exchange apparatus and the late posting box. On many vehicles the latter was a box which was hung on the outside of the carriage while it was being loaded or unloaded. Only in later vehicles was the posting slot an integral part.

Right from the early days it was seen that separate vehicles were needed for stowage as well as sorting. Communications between vehicles was a problem until 1859 when the Post Office suggested an experiment with gangways. Following success on the London & North Eastern Railway these were soon put into service on the Great Western and South Eastern railways' routes. It was soon apparent that this innovation could have a

wider application on ordinary passenger services and it was therefore copied. In February 1911 the following letter was sent from the LNWR to the Post Office:

'I now learn from our Carriage Superintendent that it is quite correct that gangways were first introduced in connection with the 'Travelling Post Office' vehicles, and eventually brought into common use for

Above right:
York-built No 80340 seen at Weymouth, where it is allocated to South Western TPO duties. Note the smaller windows and the sliding connecting door. When built this vehicle was fitted with traductors only. 31 March 1984. *Author*

Right:
The sorting frame side of No 80340. *Author*

Below:
The latest postal vehicles to be built were constructed on second-hand underframes at Wolverton in 1977. Five of the new sorting carriages, Nos 80381, 80392/3/4/5, were photographed at Holyhead on a test train on 31 May 1977. *Author*

general passenger traffic, as far as this Company is concerned.'

To make the best use of the space available in the early four-wheeled vehicles the gangways were placed off-centre. As larger and more modern vehicles entered service they retained this feature so that they could be operated with the older cars. This sometimes caused problems when stock was returned from servicing the wrong way round and arrangements had to be made to turn the vehicles concerned. It also prevented through communication with other, centre gangway, stock which might be running with the postal vehicles. This distinction was to remain until

Left:
The interior of one of the last apparatus fitted sorting coaches to be built. The roller shutter at the left secure the registered letter frames. *The Post Office (copyright reserved)*

Below:
The first BR stowage van, No 80400, as built in 1959. *H. S. Wilson Collection*

the current postal stock was introduced from 1959.

As the railway network developed the Post Office entered into agreements with each company regarding the carriage of mails. Where sorting was required the company was to provide suitable vehicles. They were not permitted to use those of another company, so when the Scottish mails reached Carlisle, for example, they had to be transferred from LNWR stock to that provided by the Caledonian Railway. This particular arrangement lasted until 1885, when the Scottish mails were accelerated, and the companies were able to co-operate in providing the West Coast Joint Stock for postal purposes.

Some details of the vehicles provided by the various companies follows, along with some notes on the vehicles which have been preserved.

British Rail

When BR was established in 1948 the postal fleet consisted mainly of vehicles built since the railway grouping of 1923. It is necessary to qualify this statement in the light of the number of pre-grouping vehicles which were still available for use in various parts of the country. The eight Southern Railway cars were supported by reserves built by the London & South Western Railway, the Midland Region was still using London &

Below:
No 80401 at Wolverton after being painted in the blue and grey livery. 22 September 1968.
D. L. Percival

Bottom:
York-built stowage van No 80438 had no provision for apparatus. It is being shunted at Derby prior to working the Derby-Bristol TPO on 23 June 1981.
C. J. Tuffs

Right:
One of the second batch of brake stowage tenders, built at York in 1968, photographed at Aberdeen on 25 October 1977. *Author*

Below right:
One of the GNR's postal twin sets; this pair was converted in 1900 from 1889 built vehicles. Apparatus was fitted on both sides.
Courtesy of the National Railway Museum, York

Bottom right:
A brake stowage tender from the brake end, showing the branding applied to the end to comply with BR's operational requirements.
The Post Office (copyright reserved)

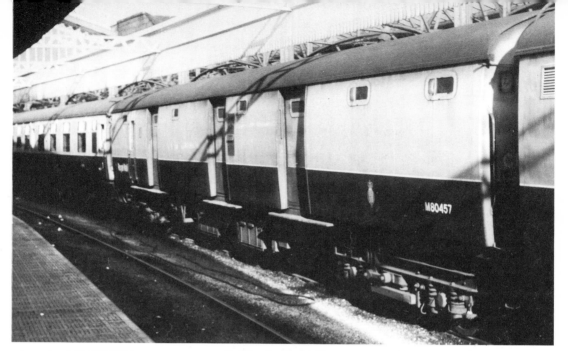

Above:
The crew of the London & Exeter RPO standing alongside GWR No 850, a 46ft 6in vehicle built in 1887. It was fitted with four traductors on the same side as the net and had gangways at each end. The late letter box would be moved inside when the vehicle was in transit. *H. S. Wilson Collection*

Below:
A combined passenger and sorting carriage. Built in 1889 with broad gauge running gear, this type was unique to the Great Western. The off-centre corridor was only fitted to the postal end.
British Rail

North Western Railway and West Coast Joint Stock vehicles and in Scotland the three cars built by the Highland Railway in 1916 were in regular use on the Highland TPO.

Where new construction was required during the 1950s the LMSR pattern of vehicle was used, 30 new coaches being built at Wolverton between 1948 and 1958. By this time steps were being taken to withdraw the older vehicles and replace them by new ones using, where possible, the designs and tech-

niques developed for the Mk 1 passenger coaching stock.

The first of the new vehicles entered service on the Great Western TPO on 19 October 1959, the GWR cars previously used being transferred to other services. Internally the new coaches were little different from their predecessors. There was, however, one major change, which arose from the decision to fit centre gangways instead of the off-centre gangways which had been a feature of so many earlier vehicles.

By 1977, 145 of the new cars had been built at Wolverton and York. There were 96 sorting vans, 40 stowage vans and nine brake stowage vans. Some of the coaches were built on the underframes of surplus passenger coaches. Some were fitted for apparatus working and some had provision for it. Because of the time span during which the vehicles were built there were other changes, too. The early construction had filament lamps and folding gangway doors, the later

Top:
This carriage was a rebuild of one like that shown in the previous picture. *British Rail*

Above:
A Great Western TPO in action, about to pick up pouches from the lineside apparatus. *British Rail*

ones had fluorescent lighting and sliding doors. A number of changes arose from the Great Train Robbery, the most noticeable being the reversion to small windows, as on the pre-nationalisation stock.

Eight stowage vans were built with flat ends and fitted with off-centre gangways so that they could work with the older vehicles then running on the Midland TPO. In 1972 this TPO was seen with one of these standard cars running with two LMS cars and one LNER car. The latter was still in the pre-1970 red livery so the whole ensemble must have looked quite a sight. Centre gangways had been fitted by 1975.

Nine brake stowage vans were built for use on the Great Western TPO and the Up and Down Specials. This enabled these trains to be made up exclusively of postal vehicles.

As mentioned earlier, until 1970 the standard TPO livery was red. This tended to vary in shade according to the works which applied it. The Southern Railway and the later Southern Region had green TPO coaches to match their coaching stock. From 1970 the

Below:
A 50ft Great Western vehicle seen at Bristol on 16 May 1959. It was built in 1933 and was fitted with electric heaters by BR so that it could be heated while standing at Bristol when working on the London-Bristol-Plymouth circuit. *J. Hodge*

Bottom:
No 849 was built in 1932 for service on the South Wales TPO. It is seen at Carmarthen, 14 September 1962. Apparatus was never fitted to this car. *P. H. Swift*

standard blue and grey has been applied, the 'Royal Mail' brand, royal crest and red letter box panel contriving to make these vehicles as distinctive as ever.

Of the 144 vehicles now in service (one was damaged beyond repair after an accident in East Anglia in 1982) up to 30 may be designated spare at any one time, excluding vehicles being serviced. This is indicative of the postal requirement to have guaranteed

Below:
No 849 seen from the opposite side. This car had a 56ft 10½in body. *P. H. Swift*

Bottom:
GWR No 807 as turned out in 1945, photographed at Old Oak Common. It was one of a batch of three built in 1929. This livery has been applied to the preserved No 814 at Didcot
The Post Office, Crown Copyright

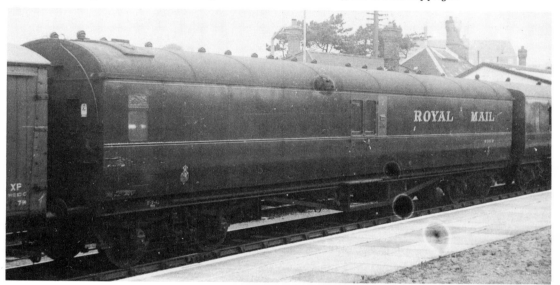

50ft bodied No 813 seen at Swindon in Southern Region green livery on 31 August 1965. This was one of three brake stowage vans built in 1933 with apparatus fitted on both sides. This allowed the Up GW TPO to pick up at Liskeard, the only apparatus point on the Up duty, without turning vehicles.
P. H. Swift

Below:
Highland Railway No 5, seen at Dingwall as LM Region M30321 on 16 May 1958.
F. W. Shuttleworth

availability. To keep track of the vehicles the TPO Section maintains an availability board in its Old Street offices.

Six brake stowage vans and 18 sorting vans are carried on standard B2 bogies, the remainder using heavyweight B4 bogies. All the stock is dual-heated and, except for the same six brake stowage vans and 18 sorting vans (which are vacuum braked only), the fleet is dual-braked. Most of the fleet is capable of operating at 100mph.

For the benefit of the staff, the vehicles have toilets, electric water heaters, ovens and wardrobes. The carriages are pressure ventilated and a great deal of effort went into providing adequate draught exclusion. To this end the gangway doors are operated electrically and close automatically 7sec after

being opened. The door-control push button is placed so that a laden postman can use his elbow to operate it. The opening of a door in one carriage automatically opens that in the adjoining vehicle.

Caledonian Railway

The Caledonian Railway's first postal carriage was built in October 1848. The company undertook the responsibility of providing the stock for the TPOs which it operated until the creation of the West Coast Joint Stock in 1879. Seven vehicles were taken over for the WCJS, which with one exception were 26ft long. Two were built by the LNWR.

Cambrian Railways

The Cambrian Railway's first sorting carriage entered service in 1888. Numbered 200, it was a 32ft long six-wheeled carriage. In 1902 it was joined by a 42ft bogie vehicle, No 293. The older car was then kept at Shrewsbury as a spare. Both survived to be re-numbered, 810-11, by the GWR.

Cornwall Railway

Initially the Cornwall Railway hired a sorting carriage from the Bristol & Exeter Railway, an arrangement which did not meet with Post Office approval. Giving way to the pressure applied, the company had its own vehicle built by Shackleford & Co in 1861. It was 28ft 3in long and had a papier mâché body. It

Left:
1916 built Highland Railway No 10 seen at The Mound on 30 July 1952. It was working the down Highland TPO (Northern Section). When new these vehicles were painted dark olive green with scarlet ends. *F. W. Shuttleworth*

Below:
London, Brighton & South Coast Railway sorting carriage No 401. This was one of three built in 1878; it was withdrawn in 1920. *H. S. Wilson Collection*

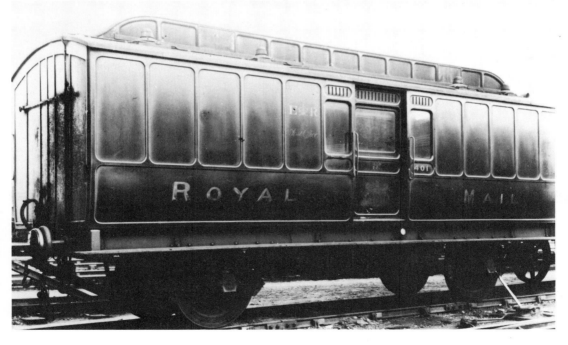

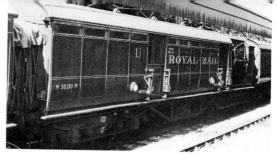

remained in service until 31 May 1892. Possibly two vehicles were also modified for postal use in 1862.

Furness Railway
The Furness Railway built two sorting carriages, No 1 in 1887 and No 2 in 1903. The former was 22ft 6in long and the latter was 32ft 6in. Prior to the construction of No 1, a secondhand vehicle of LNWR origin was used.

Great Eastern Railway
The GER built 22 postal vehicles, the first in 1890, the last in 1921. No 1 of 1890 had incandescent gas lighting and Westinghouse air brakes. Steam heating was fitted in 1912. Some of the GER vehicles were conversions from third class carriages or brakes; they were invariably 20 years old on conversion and lasted from 10 to 20 years in postal service. At the Grouping 11 vehicles passed to the LNER, three of these being conversions, which were withdrawn in October 1929, the remainder in November 1933. Unusually for TPOs, some of these coaches had centre gangways.

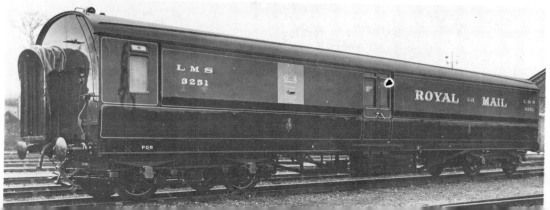

Glasgow & South Western Railway

The LMSR acquired six postal cars from the G&SWR in 1923. They were built between 1887 and 1910, three of them being six-wheelers with 31ft bodies. Prior to undertaking its own construction, the G&SWR had used Caledonian Railway stock.

Great Northern Railway

From 1871 the Great Northern Railway built about a dozen postal vehicles. They were constructed at Doncaster, three being designed by H. N. Gresley. In addition the GNR also ran a number of conversions as close-coupled twin-sets. The original six-wheeled vehicles were built c1889 and the twinning operation took place before World War 1. Some of these sets had apparatus on both sides. Most of the GNR stock had centre gangways. The LNER was to convert some GNR brakes for postal use in 1929; this work was done at Stratford.

Great North of Scotland Railway

This railway built two 27ft sorting carriages in 1886. They had no gangways and lighting was by oil lamps. The spare was a 20ft carriage purchased from the LNWR.

Great Western Railway

The first postal vehicles provided by the GWR were bag tenders, used from 1844. They were built to the broad gauge and weighed just over 7ton. Carriages with a length of 46ft 6in were built in 1883 which were suitable for conversion to standard gauge. Four four-wheeled postal brakes were built in 1891 and 1892. By 1907 they were all in service as passenger brakes. After the gauge conversion of 1892 the GWR built postal stock of three basic styles; clerestory roofed stock until 1903, elliptical roofed 68ft/70ft stock until 1910 and steel panelled stock from 1927 to 1947. Most of the latter were 57ft vehicles, 10 were 50ft, four were 63ft and three were 46ft 6in. On the Ocean Mails run from Plymouth the GWR slipped a postal car at Bedminster; it was then worked to Bristol. When the first BR standard coaches were introduced to the Great Western TPO in 1959,

Below:
No 30214 was also built in 1931 but had no toilet compartment. Aberdeen, 2 August 1966.
P. H. Swift

Bottom:
No 30204 was built in 1934. Apart from the length of 57ft and lack of toilet facilities it was the same as No 3251, shown in the previous photographs. It was the only vehicle built to diagram 1908.
British Rail

54

the GW cars were transferred away from their home territory for further use. Some went to the London Midland Region for use on the Specials and some moved to the Southern Region as reserves for the ex-Southern Railway vehicles. Others went to the North Eastern Region.

Highland Railway

The Highland Railway's list of postal stock ran to 14 vehicles but there was undoubtedly some duplication as new carriages took the numbers of withdrawn vehicles. Nos 1, 2 and 4 were 27ft 6in four-wheelers. No 3 was a 49ft 6in Post Office parcel van built in 1901. Nos 7, 8 and 9 were six-wheeled cars scrapped in 1916-7. Nos 11 and 12 were also six-wheeled cars and had 23ft 6in bodies. Nos 13 and 14 replaced similarly numbered older vehicles, probably in 1914, and were 41ft bogie cars. In 1916 the railway built three new 49ft 6in bogie vehicles, numbered 5, 6 and 10. They had matchboard sides and

remained in use until 1961. It is said that they had their origins in a general arrangement drawing obtained from the LNWR, although this is not betrayed by their appearance. The original Nos 5, 6 and 10 became passenger luggage vans and then, in LMSR days, tool vans. Nine vehicles passed to the LMS in 1923, but only four remained to be re-numbered in 1933.

London, Brighton & South Coast Railway

Four sorting carriages, 26ft long, were built in 1878. Two were withdrawn in 1899 and one

Below:
Being built in 1936, sorting carriage No 30230 was possibly the only vehicle to carry the monogram of King Edward VIII when new. *British Rail*

Bottom:
No 30249, built a year later, received the monogram of King George VI. Like No 30230 it was nominally the same as No 3251 but there are some differences, noticeably on the roofline. *British Rail*

in 1920. Two 48ft carriages were built at Brighton in 1897. They became brake/luggage vans in 1921 and were withdrawn in 1931 and 1933. All six vehicles had clerestory roofs.

London, Chatham & Dover Railway

Two sorting carriages entered service on the LCDR in 1893. The 32ft bodies were mounted on six-wheeled underframes. One was withdrawn in 1917, the other in 1930.

London, Midland & Scottish Railway

From 1929 68 postal carriages were built to LMSR designs. All were built at Wolverton, the same works which produced the LNWR and WCJS fleets. Most of the LMSR stock had 60ft bodies, but some were 50ft or 57ft. Two short bodied vans, 42ft and 31ft, were built in 1933; the shorter ran on six wheels and was transferred to parcels duties in 1952, and withdrawn in 1965. The first withdrawls from the main fleet were made in 1948, the last been withdrawn by 1978. Thirteen LMSR designed vehicles were transferred to other regions towards the end of their operational lives.

The LMSR inherited a large collection of postal vehicles from its constituent companies in 1923. Some of these were very long lived and survived to see service with British Rail, a few even receiving the blue and grey livery.

Below left:
The interior of No 30249. The sorting frames were built to different dimensions for sorting letters, packets, newspapers and registered items.
British Rail

Below:
No 30289 followed No 30249 in 1939. It was a 60ft vehicle without apparatus, although this could have been fitted subsequently. *British Rail*

Above right:
Built after the war, in 1947, sorting carriage No 30292 had no provision for apparatus on its 60ft body. *British Rail*

Right:
No 30292 seen from the sorting frame side. In 1971 this vehicle was on the Midland TPO duty. *British Rail*

Below right:
No 30275 was built by British Railways in 1950. It was a 60ft stowage van with a guard's compartment and toilet facilities. At 9ft 2¼in wide it was 8¼in wider than the majority of LMSR vehicles. *British Rail*

London & North Eastern Railway

As with the later Great Northern Railway vehicles, the LNER postal stock was built to the distinctive designs of Nigel Gresley. The first entered traffic in 1929. Over the years 24 vehicles were built at York and Doncaster. The last seven cars were steel (instead of teak) panelled, six of them being built under BR auspices in 1949. One of the steel-panelled cars, built in 1946, had a 52ft 6in body, the rest of the fleet being 60ft 1½in vehicles. The last LNER postal vehicles withdrawn from service, in 1975, were the steel-panelled type.

In the 1920s and 30s the LNER converted 10 former North Eastern Railway and Great Northern Railway vehicles for postal use on the Great Eastern section. The last of these was withdrawn in 1950.

London & North Western Railway

The history of the LNWR postal stock is highly complex. The first vehicles were built following the Grand Junction Railway TPO experiment in 1838, and 11 vehicles were in use by 1846. One of these survived until 1885 when the Post Office complained about it being used on the Manchester-Crewe service. Some of them, possibly all, were 22ft 6in six-wheeled coaches. More postal stock was built, in 1854 and 1855, with 20ft bodies. In 1879 steps were taken to improve the Scottish mails so the LNWR co-operated with the Caledonian Railway to provide a

Left:
Sorting tender No 30298 was also built in 1950. It was photographed on the Highland TPO at Inverness in 1976. *Author*

Below left:
The last LMS style vehicle, No 30309, was turned out from Wolverton works in 1958. When new it was allocated to the Whitehaven-Preston TPO. *The Post Office, Crown Copyright*

Above right:
A publicity photograph of sorting on the Down Special TPO in 1954. *British Rail*

Right:
The interior of an LMS stowage van in use on the Specials. The photograph was taken in 1948. *The Post Office (copyright reserved)*

Below:
Handling the mails at Euston before the LMSR design stock was withdrawn. *British Rail*

Below:

The end of the line. Two LMSR stowage vans used as a store and a canteen at a packing case factory in Leicester since 1978. No 30305, nearest the camera, is a 57ft vehicle built in 1954. The second one is 30279, a 60ft vehicle of 1950 vintage: it was in use on the Midland TPO in September 1970 and was apparatus fitted when built. *Author*

Below:

No 2286 was built in York in 1929 as one of the first LNER postal vehicles. Initially allocated to the North Eastern TPO, it was re-allocated to the East Anglian TPO from July 1932; the apparatus was removed at the same time. This stock remained in service until 1966/7.
Courtesy of the National Railway Museum, York

Bottom left:

The LNER commissioned its photographer to take a series of a postal car under construction at York. It started with the bare frames and ended with the completed vehicle. In addition to the postal equipment these vehicles had overhead heating and a lavatory and a wardrobe for staff.
Courtesy of the National Railway Museum, York

Bottom:

This view, from the same series, shows the net aperture before the roof was constructed.
Courtesy of the National Railway Museum, York

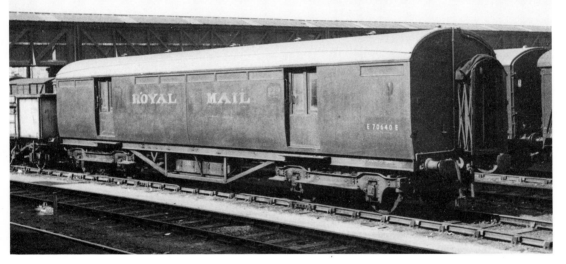

pool of rolling stock for these services. The pool was to be managed by the West Coast Joint Stock committee to whom the LNWR transferred nine postal vehicles. These were up to 25 years old and, with three exceptions, were 22ft 6in long. The remainder were 26ft and 32ft long. The LNWR resumed ownership of some of this stock, and took on some of Caledonian origin, when they were no longer required by the WCJS. Postal stock was still required by the LNWR for its English and Irish services for which five 32ft vehicles were provided in 1891. By 1899 the railway had 14 32ft carriages in service. At the Grouping 34 vehicles of 42ft and 50ft length were transferred to the LMSR.

Top:
This LNER stowage van entered service in 1949; it was converted from a 51ft 1½in brake van.
D. Ibbotson/F. W. Shuttleworth Collection

Above:
The only steel-panelled LNER stowage van, No 70640, was built in 1946 at Doncaster. It had a 52ft 4in body and was photographed at Gloucester Eastgate on 23 March 1963. *P. H. Swift*

London & South Western Railway

From 1881 to 1914, 18 postal carriages were built for service on the LSWR. By 1892 five had been built with 32ft bodies on six-wheel underframes: the last of these was withdrawn in 1933. The remaining bogie

Top:
LNWR No 20, now preserved, seen in the scrap line at Wolverton on 3 May 1959. Its post-1933 LMSR number, also used by BR, was 30244.
F. W. Shuttleworth

Above:
LNWR No 9235 in its BR guise, as No 30243, at Workington. 7 May 1954. *F. W. Shuttleworth*

Right:
LNWR No 35 was to become LMSR/BR No 30252.
Author's Collection

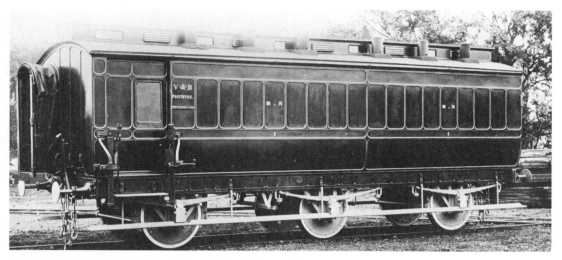

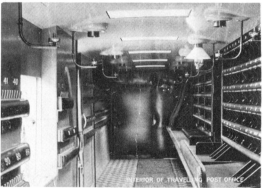

Above:
Midland Railway No 1, built in 1879. It was 30ft long and had no gangway at the right-hand end. *British Rail*

Left:
The interior of an LNWR sorting carriage. The pegs on the left were for hanging partially full bags of mail. *Author's Collection*

Below left:
This 1886 built LSWR vehicle ended its postal career as SR No 4904 prior to being converted for service use. It is shown at Fullerton Junction in May 1955. *M. Rhodes*

War the Southern's postal services were withdrawn so several postal vehicles were put to departmental use from 1942. Three cars passed to British Railways in 1948 and remained in service until circa 1960. Some LSWR postal cars remained in departmental service during the 1950s.

Midland Railway
The first Midland Railway TPO vehicles entered service in 1845. They were similar to the contemporary London & Birmingham Railway vehicles, being built by the same builder in Birmingham. Two more carriages were built in 1850 and a further two in 1852. The last two were jointly owned by the Midland, the York & North Midland, the York, Newcastle & Berwick and the North British Railways, probably because they ran as bag tenders between Newcastle, where connection was made with the Midland TPO, and Edinburgh. Three vehicles built in 1857 were

stock varied in length between 44ft and 56ft. The whole fleet passed to the Southern Railway in 1923 and the new management made the first withdrawals in 1928. During the 1930s seven cars received 'new' underframes from South Eastern & Chatham Railway vehicles. In 1940 an 1898 LSWR postal car was converted to become an ARP lecture theatre; previously No 4911 it then became No 1448S. During the War the Southern's postal services were

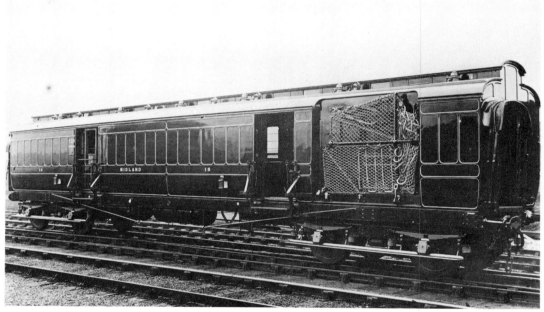

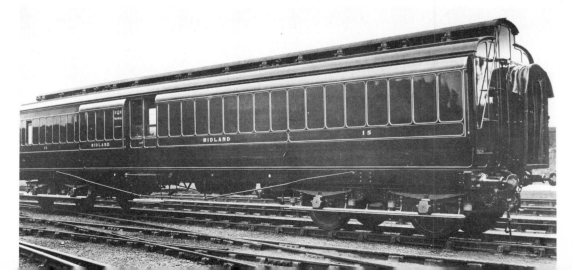

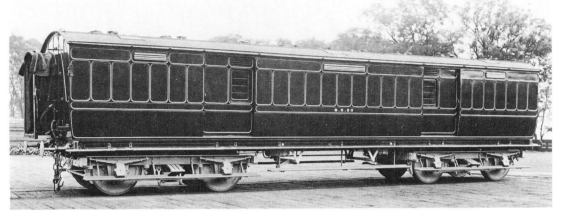

Above left:
Midland Railway No 8 was built in 1888. It had no net but had two traductors. Gangways were fitted at both ends of the 43ft body. *British Rail*

Left:
Midland Railway No 15 entered service on the Derby-Bristol TPO in 1907. *British Rail*

Below left:
The opposite side of MR No 15. It was fitted with sorting frames but some space was allocated for stowage. The body was 54ft long. *British Rail*

Above:
Built in 1885 for parcel sorting on the Midland TPO, No 80 was 43ft long. *British Rail*

Below:
The remains of a Midland Railway postal car seen at Shepton Mallet on 2 October 1965. *P. H. Swift*

Below right:
Built in 1879, at the same time as Midland Railway No 1, No 5 is seen here branded for the Midland and North Eastern Joint Postal Stock, although in 1895 it was allocated to the Derby & St Pancras ST. *British Rail*

owned solely by the Midland but the North Eastern Railway made a contribution towards their cost. The first of a number of six-wheeled vehicles was built in 1858. A further nine, with 30ft bodies, entered service in 1859. In 1885 two 43ft vehicles were built, then one in 1886, two in 1888, one in 1893 and a further one in 1896. Three 32ft vehicles were also added to the roster in 1885.

The nine 54ft vehicles built in 1907 were the last postal stock to be built by the Midland. All stock used on the Midland TPO was jointly owned by the North Eastern Railway and operated as the Midland & North Eastern Joint Postal Stock. The joint operation continued after the Grouping when the partners were the LMSR and the LNER. The vehicles which were used on the Bristol-Derby and the Lincoln-Tamworth services were wholly owned by the Midland Railway.

North British Railway
The first postal vehicles to enter service on the

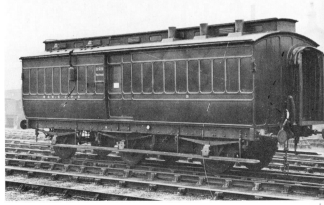

Top:
No 5 was fitted with a full set of exchange apparatus. *British Rail*

Above:
No 16 built in 1879 and its crew. In 1895 this sorting carriage was allocated to the Midland TPO as the branding indicates. It was only gangwayed at one end. *F. W. Shuttleworth Collection*

North British Railway were bag tenders, in 1853. They were fitted with apparatus in August 1861 and replaced by new sorting carriages the following month. By 1895 three 23ft 7in carriages had been acquired from the North Eastern Railway. A 28ft 6in vehicle

had been built in 1882. A 32ft carriage built in 1887 was withdrawn in 1915. A further 32ft carriage entered service in 1891. A 52ft car was built in 1904 and a 51ft vehicle followed in 1905.

North Eastern Railway
The operation of the Midland & North Eastern Joint Postal Stock in conjunction with the Midland TPO was the North Eastern Railway's greatest involvement with postal services. A small fleet of TPO carriages was maintained for local services. A 22ft 9in vehicle of 1897 was later close coupled to a 24ft vehicle of 1873 and the two operated as a pair. Vehicles of 23ft 7in were built in 1872

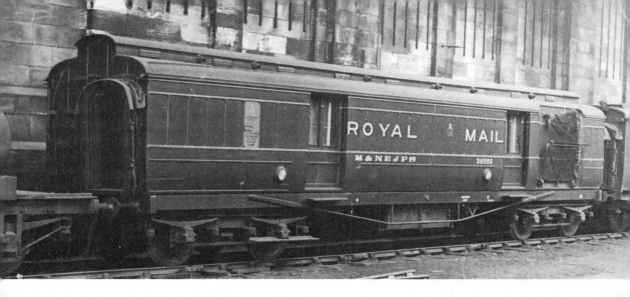

Top:
This vehicle, from the same batch as No 15, already illustrated, still carried its JPS branding when photographed at Carlisle on 27 April 1949.
H. C. Casserley

Above:
The North Eastern Railway's largest postal vehicle was built at York in 1903 and was 52ft long. Extra space was created internally by flaring the side panels to accommodate the sorting frames. Apparatus was fitted on the opposite side.
Courtesy of the National Railway Museum, York

Right:
A South Eastern & Chatham Railway postal carriage relegated to use as a store at Lancing Works. Photographed 16 March 1960.
E. Wilmshurst/H. S. Wilson Collection

and 1876 and later sold to the North British Railway. A 52ft carriage was built in 1903 with gas lighting, a net and four traductors.

South Eastern & Chatham Railway

In addition to operating the stock of its constituent companies, the London, Chatham & Dover and the South Eastern Railways, the SE&CR ran a fleet of 10 postal vehicles built under its own auspices. Three 50ft 1in sorting carriages entered service in 1904, followed by two more in 1906. Five similar stowage vans were built in 1907. All 10 cars passed to the Southern Railway in 1923, when the stowage vans were classified as luggage vans. Three of them were restored to postal service in 1931. The sorting carriages and the reprieved stowage vans all saw service with BR until withdrawal in 1960 and 1961. It is interesting to note the constructional details of these vehicles which had a teak body frame with mahogany panels; the underframe had

wooden headstocks, channel iron bolster cross-bars and iron end longitudinals, the rest was oak.

South Eastern Railway

By 1896 the SER had built 13 postal carriages. The oldest was a four-wheeler built in 1855, three more four-wheelers were built in 1866 and 1868. The 1855 vehicle was transferred to departmental use in 1902. The others were withdrawn in 1906. Five six-wheelers were built in 1859-60 and 1863;

four were withdrawn in 1906, the fifth had already been in departmental service since 1902. Two more six-wheeled vehicles were built in 1881 and 1883; they passed to the Southern Railway and were withdrawn in 1933. The only bogie vehicles were 44ft stowage vans built in 1896. In 1939 one of these, No 4947, became an ARP instruction coach, the other passed to departmental service a year later; as Mess & Tool Van No 15375 it remained in use until 1961.

Left:
The first Southern Railway sorting carriage, No 4919, seen at Weymouth on 7 September 1963. *P. H. Swift*

Below left:
The 1939-built vehicles had the door placed differently, as seen in this photograph of No 4921. Swindon Carriage & Wagon Works, 8 May 1964. *P. H. Swift*

Above right:
The opposite side of No 4921. This vehicle was used on the last run of the South Eastern TPO on 18 February 1977. *P. H. Swift*

Right:
Southern Railway stowage van No 4960 seen at Weymouth, 7 September 1963. Its duty was the South Western TPO. *P. H. Swift*

Below:
West Coast Joint Stock No 187 of 1883; the Webb designed radial trucks are clearly seen. This 42ft carriage was destroyed in an accident at Willesden in 1899. *Author's Collection*

Above:
WCJS No 348 was built in 1886 and allocated to the Glasgow Section of the Up Special TPO when new. A radial axle was fitted to one end.
H. S. Wilson Collection

Right:
Another view of No 348, showing the corridor connection. Numbered 3243 by the LMSR in 1923, this 32ft carriage was withdrawn in 1931.
H. S. Wilson Collection

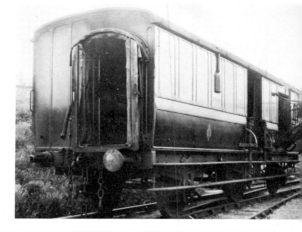

Below:
No 437 was built for the WCJS at Wolverton in 1910. A 57ft carriage, it was damaged in an accident at Kirtlebridge in 1916, repaired and finally withdrawn in 1951. Its BR number was 30200. *British Rail*

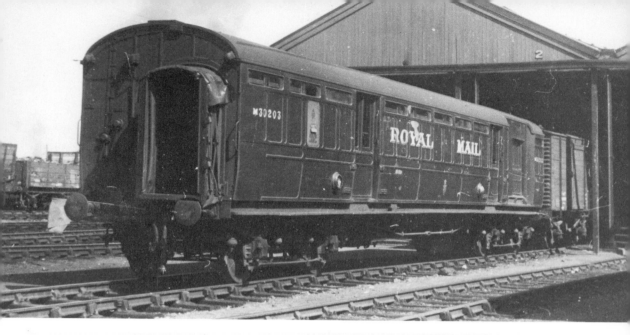

Southern Railway

The postal stock inherited by the SR in 1923 has already been mentioned. As the railway only operated postal routes to Dover and Dorchester a large fleet was not required; the pre-grouping vehicles were reasonably long lived, so it was not necessary for the company to consider providing replacements until the 1930s. The prototype sorting carriage was built at Eastleigh in 1936. Three more similar vehicles appeared in 1939; differences included the provision of a toilet. Four stowage vans also appeared in 1939. All eight vehicles had 58ft bodies. One of the stowage vans was allocated to the Dover service, the remainder to the Dorchester run. The operating pattern remained the same after British

Railways took over in 1948. The first withdrawal, a stowage van, took place in 1962. The last duty for these vehicles was on the South Eastern TPO; when this finished on 18 February 1977 the last ones in service were withdrawn. Three of them were to be preserved.

West Coast Joint Stock

In 1879 the LNWR and the Caledonian Railway agreed to pool sufficient postal stock to permit the London-Aberdeen duties to be worked by the same stock throughout. The LNWR supplied nine cars, the Caledonian seven. From 1881 new stock was specially built at Wolverton. A total of 75 postal vehicles had been built, to 23 different diagrams, by 1922. The earliest coaches had 26ft bodies, the latest, built in 1917, measured 64ft. As the LMSR absorbed both WCJS partners the joint stock ceased to be operated separately from 1923. The WCJS passed 41 postal cars to the new organisation; the last was withdrawn by British Rail in 1965.

In 1888 Wolverton built two special WCJS vehicles which were not to enter service. They were one-sixth full-size scale models of 32ft and 42ft sorting carriages and were built for the German postal museum in Berlin. Their fate is not known.

Preservation

The number of TPO vehicles in preservation is very small; it is not possible, for example, to tell the story of TPO vehicle development through the vehicles existing, and many interesting types have been lost. Constructional details were often common to the story of carriage development and can therefore be seen in other vehicles which have been saved. In essence, though, there have only been two types of TPO vehicle; the sorting van and the stowage van, both of which may be seen in an operational condition on preservation sites.

None of the four- and six-wheel TPO

Below:
The replica of the Grand Junction Railway sorting carriage is now kept at the National Railway Museum, York. *British Rail*

Above right:
With its net removed, No 30311 stood at Carlisle on 18 September 1956. As WCJS No 184, this 50ft vehicle was built in 1900. It was withdrawn in 1958. *F. W. Shuttleworth*

Right:
Also kept at the National Railway Museum is West Coast Joint Stock No 186, built in 1883. The LMSR restored it for display at the TPO centenary exhibition in 1938. *British Rail*

Below right:
The interior of WCJS No 186. *British Rail*

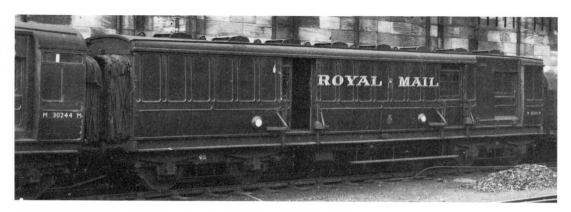

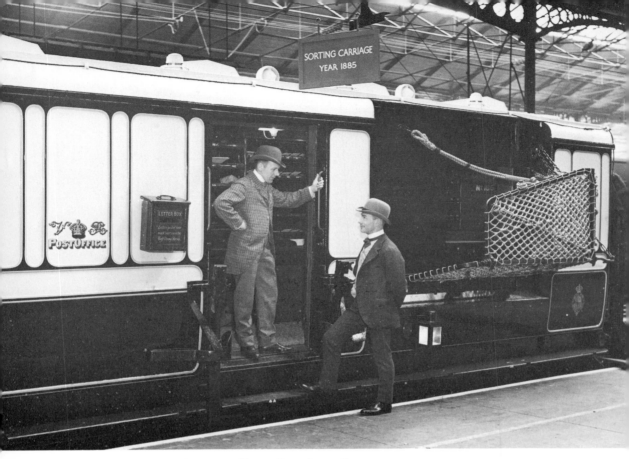

SORTING CARRIAGE
YEAR 1885

LETTER BOX

POST OFFICE

vehicles has survived. Some idea of early construction may be obtained from the replica Grand Junction Railway coach built by the LMSR for the TPO centenary celebrations in 1938. Until it went on display at the Museum of British Transport, at Clapham, it was stored at Wolverton Works. Since 1975 it has been on show at the National Railway Museum in York.

Another survivor from the TPO centenary exhibition also on display at York is the West Coast Joint Stock No 186, which was built for the accelerated Scottish services of 1885. It was withdrawn and restored to 1885 condition, complete with a Webb radial truck, especially for the exhibition. It has four axles, the inner two fixed and the outer ones being allowed to move according to the curvature of the track. It is the oldest surviving British TPO vehicle.

Built in 1909, London & North Western Railway No 20 was renumbered 9520 by the LNWR and 3227 and 30244 by the LMSR. The latter number, allocated in 1933, lasted

Above:
No 186 at the Euston exhibition.
The Post Office (copyright reserved)

Top right:
The lineside apparatus shown at the Great Western Society's depot at Didcot. *Author*

Above right:
LMSR sorting carriage No 30225 at the Midland Railway Trust's premises at Butterley, Derbyshire.
Paul Brindley/Midland Railway Trust

Right:
LNER sorting carriage No 70294 under restoration at the Great Central Railway, Loughborough, Leicestershire. *Author*

until the vehicle was withdrawn in 1961. It was used on the Irish services until 1940 and its apparatus was removed in 1945. After withdrawal it was acquired by the Railway Preservation Society and taken to their base at Chasewater, Staffordshire, where it housed the small relics collection. In 1983 it was moved to the Tyseley depot of the Birming-

ham Railway Museum. It is now owned by the BRM which intends to restore the vehicle and establish a working TPO demonstration.

The Great Western Railway is represented by No 814, a sorting van built in 1940 to replace an identical vehicle which was destroyed in an accident that year. Following the introduction of BR standard stock on the Great Western TPO in 1959, No 814 was transferred to the Southern Region as a spare for the South Western TPO workings. When the standard stock reached these duties in

1972 it became surplus to postal requirements and was transfered to departmental service. Becoming surplus again, it was sold to the Great Western Society in June 1975. The GWS had erected lineside apparatus alongside its demonstration line at Didcot in 1973. The coach was put through a comprehensive restoration programme but it was not until 11 August 1979 that the apparatus was tested and was first demonstrated to the

public on 29 September 1979. The mail exchange is now a popular feature of the Society's open days.

The only combination of sorting and stowage vans to be preserved together originated with the London & North Eastern Railway. The set belongs to Railway Vehicle Preservations Ltd, who acquired the stowage van, No 70268, in 1973.

Around 1960 it was converted to become a PO stowage van, based at Newcastle. The sorting van, No 70294, was built as No 2441 at York in 1937. It was used on East Coast Main Line services until the 1960s when it was transferred to East Anglia; the apparatus net was removed at this time but the traductors remained in use for putting down mail at Manningtree. The author has a record of seeing this vehicle in service on the London-Norwich bag tender in November 1972. It was sold in 1974 and bought by RVP who moved it to join the stowage van at Rye House Power Station. By 1976 both had been moved to the Stour Valley Railway at Chappel & Wakes Colne Station in Essex. They moved again, in June 1981, to the Great Central Railway in Leicestershire. Work started on restoration to operational condition immediately and arrangements were made to instal the ground apparatus, owned since 1974, at Quorn & Woodhouse station. Tests were carried out in the first week of May 1982 and the first public demonstration took place on the eighth of that month. The Leicester Post Office supplied postmen in vintage uniforms and a special postmark was applied to the mail which was put through the apparatus.

A sorting van, No 30225, was built at Wolverton works by the London, Midland &

Below:
The lineside apparatus at Quorn & Woodhouse station. Note the net folded back, away from the track when not in use. *Author*

Bottom:
The first public run, with the train hauled by 'Director' No 506 *Butler Henderson.* **8 May 1982.** *Author*

Scottish Railway in 1939 and saw service on the Up and Down Specials and the North Western TPO until 1968. Its nets were then removed and it was transferred to the Manchester-Glasgow SC duty. Purchased by Derby Corporation after withdrawal in 1973 it is now to be seen at the Midland Railway Trust's Centre at Butterley, Derbyshire. Before the Trust opened its line the TPO vehicle served as a museum at Butterley. It is now on show at Swanwick and may be restored to working order as the Trust does own both ground and carriage apparatus.

Above:
A postman in vintage uniform posing with No 70294 on 8 May 1982. *Leicester Mercury*

A similar LMSR sorting carriage, the only obvious difference being the provision of a toilet compartment, No 30272, is owned by the National Railway Museum. It was built at Wolverton by BR to an LMSR design in 1950. It was withdrawn from service in 1973 and placed in store until the summer of 1984 when it was transferred to the Birmingham Railway Museum. It is to be restored to working order and will allow an interesting comparison to be made with the Wolverton-built LNWR vehicle on the same site.

Of the seven TPO carriages built by the Southern Railway in 1939, three have been preserved. No 4920 is a sorting van; allocated to the South Western TPO until 1972, it was then transferred for use on the South Eastern TPO. It was withdrawn when this service finished in 1977 and is now owned by the National Railway Museum. It is on loan to the Nene Valley Railway at Wansford, Cambridgeshire, and has been fitted out as a museum.

Sorting van No 4922 had a similar service history to No 4920 but actually ran in service on 18 February 1977, the last night of the

Bottom:
LNWR No 20 displayed by the turntable at the Birmingham Railway Museum.
Alan Wood/Birmingham Railway Museum

Below:
Southern Railway No 4922 at the Bluebell Railway's Horsted Keynes station. *C. Burnham*

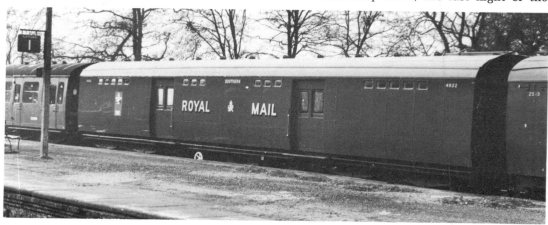

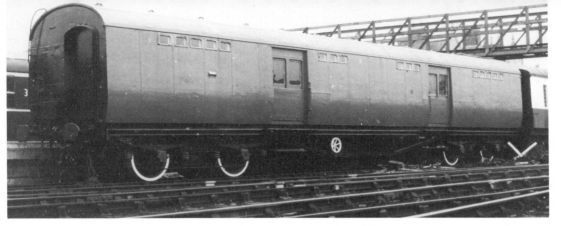

South Eastern TPO. It is now based at Horsted Keynes on the Bluebell Railway. It is sometimes run in special trains run in conjunction with the railway letter service.

Stowage van No 4958 also has a history which matches the other preserved Southern Railway vehicles. Upon withdrawal it was bought by the Mid Hants Railway and is to be seen at Ropley where it has been incorporated into a workshop.

4 Current TPO Services

This list is based on information kindly supplied by the TPO Section and is correct to April 1984. Principal staging points are included, with times for the more important. The times rarely change by more than a few minutes from timetable to timetable. Other intermediate stops are shown on the diagram. The times of these are generally available, by telephone, from the Mails Office of the Head Post Office of the location concerned.

Letters can be posted on all TPOs but collectors and enthusiasts should take care not to intrude upon, or delay, the operational function of a TPO. The public are not permitted to enter TPOs. If intending to spend several hours at a large station to look at TPOs it is advisable to hold a valid rail ticket; alternatively written permission from the station manager of the station concerned should be sought. Such precautions are worthwhile if accosted by railway police; they are naturally intrigued by anyone taking what appears to them to be an unhealthy interest in the TPOs.

A few TPOs still convey passenger portions; they are indicated in the list. Also shown are the relevant timetable numbers from the British Rail passenger timetable.

Details of the dispersal of rolling stock are shown for each duty.

Photographing TPOs is not usually allowed; it may be possible to obtain permission in advance of a proposed visit by writing to the station manager concerned. Photography on TPOs is *not* permitted.

Bristol-Derby Travelling Post Office
Bristol (d 01.10), Gloucester, Birmingham (a 03.45, d 04.12), Derby (a 05.13). Stock stabled at Derby.

Caledonian Travelling Post Office Day Down
Carlisle (d 20.50), Carstairs, Motherwell, Perth (a 00.01). Passenger train throughout, Table 65. Stock works up and down alternate nights.

Caledonian Travelling Post Office Day Up
Perth (d 21.11), Coatbridge, Carstairs, Carlisle (a 00.37). Stock works up and down alternate nights.

Caledonian Travelling Post Office Day Up (Edinburgh Section)
Edinburgh (d 21.45). Coupled to the Caledonian TPO Up at Carstairs for the journey to Carlisle. Stock returns, with the Glasgow Section coach, to Edinburgh as the Carlisle — Edinburgh SC.

Above right:
The Peterborough-Crewe TPO at Leicester in November 1983. The letters 'NSX' over the number indicate that the vehicle is a dual-braked sorting carriage. The code for stowage vans is NT and for brake stowage vans, NU. For vacuum braked vehicles the code V is added. These codes are not universally applied to the vehicles in the manner shown here. *Author*

Right:
Loading the Great Western TPO at Paddington. *Ian Allan Library*

Caledonian Travelling Post Office Day Up (Glasgow Section)
Glasgow (d 21.40). Coupled to the Caledonian TPO Up at Carstairs for the journey to Carlisle. Stock returns, with the Edinburgh Section coach, to Edinburgh as the Carlisle-Edinburgh SC.

Cardiff-Crewe Travelling Post Office
Cardiff (d 20.00), Newport (a 20.13, d 20.21), Hereford, Shrewsbury (a 22.17, d 22.25), Crewe (a 23.07). Passenger train throughout, Table 87. Stock returns to Cardiff as the Crewe-Cardiff TPO.

Carlisle-Edinburgh Sorting Carriage
Carlisle (d 02.20), Carstairs, Edinburgh (a 04.20). Added to the Down Special TPO at Carlisle and detached at Carstairs. One car remains at Edinburgh to form the Edinburgh Section of the following night's Caledonian TPO Up, the other travels to Glasgow ECS and becomes the following night's Caledonian TPO Up (Glasgow Section).

Crewe-Cardiff Travelling Post Office
Crewe (d 02.04), Shrewsbury (a 02.38, d 02.48), Hereford, Newport (a 04.46, d 04.56), Cardiff (a 05.14). Stock stabled at Cardiff.

Above:
The Great Western TPO at Penzance. 1 August 1975. *Brian Morrison*

Above right:
The up North Eastern TPO at York, showing some of the other vehicles in the train in addition to the postal stock. 13 April 1984. *Michael J. Collins*

Right:
The Norwich-London TPO at Ipswich, 24 October 1977. *Author*

Crewe-Glasgow Sorting Carriage
Crewe (d 00.01), Preston (a 00.49, d 00.58), Carlisle (a 02.09. d 02.20), Carstairs, Glasgow (a 04.00). Stock is part of the Down Special TPO from Euston; at Crewe its function changes to become the Crewe-Glasgow SC. It returns south as part of the Glasgow section of the Up Special TPO the following night.

Crewe-Peterborough Travelling Post Office
Crewe (d 00.44), Stoke-on-Trent, Derby (a 01.55, d 02.10), Leicester, Peterborough (a 04.02). Stock stabled at Peterborough.

Crewe-Peterborough Travelling Post Office (Lincoln Section)
Derby (d 02.16), Nottingham, Newark,

Lincoln (a 04.04). Detached from the Crewe-Peterborough TPO at Derby. Stock stabled at Lincoln.

Derby-Bristol Travelling Post Office
Derby (d 20.10), Birmingham (a 21.07, d 21.37), Gloucester, Bristol (a 23.53). Stock returns to Derby as Bristol-Derby TPO.

Down Special Travelling Post Office
London, Euston (d 20.35), Birmingham (a 22.18, d 22.37), Crewe (a 23.38, d 00.01), Preston (a 00.49, d 00.58), Carlisle (a 02.09, d 02.20), Carstairs, Perth (a 05.16, d 05.25), Aberdeen (a 07.20). Conveys stock which becomes the Crewe-Glasgow SC, operational from Crewe and detached at Carstairs. The stock of the Aberdeen portion becomes the following night's Up Special TPO.

East Anglian Travelling Post Office Down
London, Liverpool Street (d 23.00), Ipswich (a 00.40, d 01.50), Norwich (a 02.49). Passenger train to Ipswich, Table 11. Peterborough section detached at Ipswich. Stock works up and down alternate nights.

East Anglian Travelling Post Office Down (Peterborough Section)
Ipswich (d 01.01), Ely, Peterborough

(a 03.09), Detached from the down East
Anglian TPO at Ipswich, Stock works up and
down alternate nights.

East Anglian Travelling Post Office Up
Norwich (d 23.45), Ipswich (a 00.55,
d 02.05), London, Liverpool Street (a 03.55).
Peterborough section added at Ipswich. Stock
works up and down alternate nights.

East Anglian Travelling Post Office Up
(Peterborough Section)
Peterborough (d 23.20), Ely, Ipswich
(a 01.38). Added to the up East Anglian TPO

Top:
**The Up Special TPO passing Larbert, 9 August
1965.** *P. H. Swift*

Above:
**The Up Special TPO approaching Stanley Junction
on 31 May 1966. The rolling stock is of LMSR
construction.** *C. W. R. Bowman*

Right:
**The working of TPO stock is often interlinked and
can be very complicated, as is demonstrated by
this diagram which relates to the Specials.**
D. C. Holliday/P. M. Rees/G. P. Roberts

84

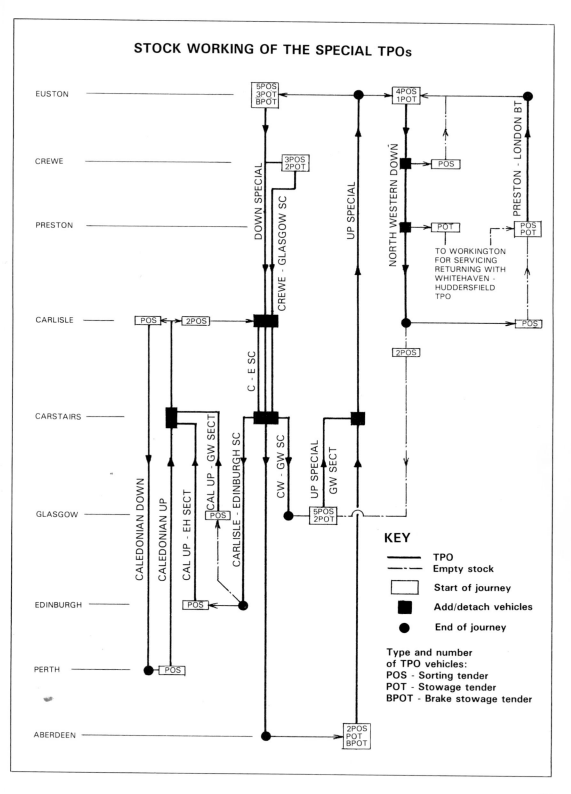

STOCK WORKING OF THE SPECIAL TPOs

EUSTON

CREWE

PRESTON

CARLISLE

CARSTAIRS

GLASGOW

EDINBURGH

PERTH

ABERDEEN

5POS
3POT
BPOT

3POS
2POT

4POS
1POT

POS

POT

TO WORKINGTON
FOR SERVICING
RETURNING WITH
WHITEHAVEN -
HUDDERSFIELD
TPO

POS
POT

POS

DOWN SPECIAL

CREWE - GLASGOW SC

UP SPECIAL

NORTH WESTERN DOWN

PRESTON - LONDON BT

C - E SC

2POS

POS

2POS

POS

CALEDONIAN DOWN

CALEDONIAN UP

CAL UP - EH SECT

CAL UP - GW SECT

CARLISLE - EDINBURGH SC

CW - GW SC

UP SPECIAL
GW SECT

POS

5POS
2POT

POS

POS

2POS
POT
BPOT

KEY

——— TPO

—·—·— Empty stock

☐ Start of journey

■ Add/detach vehicles

● End of journey

Type and number
of TPO vehicles:
POS - Sorting tender
POT - Stowage tender
BPOT - Brake stowage tender

at Ipswich. Stock works up and down alternate nights.

Edinburgh-York Travelling Post Office
Edinburgh (d 20.30), Newcastle (a 22.44, d 23.16), York (a 00.37). Stock conveyed to Newcastle with down NE TPO for adding to the following night's up North Eastern TPO.

Great Western Travelling Post Office Down
London, Paddington (d 22.25), Bristol (a 00.35, d 00.58), Plymouth, Penzance (a 06.25). Stock works up and down alternate nights.

Great Western Travelling Post Office Up
Penzance (d 19.27), Plymouth, Bristol (a 00.32, d 01.00), London, Paddington (a 03.50). Stock works up and down alternate nights.

Huddersfield-Whitehaven Travelling Post Office
Huddersfield (d 01.06), Preston (a 02.20, d 04.00), Carnforth, Barrow-in-Furness, Whitehaven (a 07.09). Stock stabled at Workington.

Above:
BR-built rolling stock is seen in this photograph of the Up Special TPO at Drumlithie on 28 March 1974. *Brian Morrison*

Right:
The first of the four passenger carriages which are permitted to be conveyed with the Up Special TPO between Aberdeen and Perth is just visible in this view taken near Cove Bay, 27 March 1974. *Brian Morrison*

London-York-Edinburgh Travelling Post Office
London, King's Cross (d 20.20), Peterborough (a 21.29, d 21.46), York (a 00.01, d 00.17), Newcastle (a 01.36, d 01.52), Edinburgh (a 04.13). At Newcastle the stowage tender is detached and forms part of the following night's up North Eastern TPO. The sorting carriage continues to Edinburgh; it returns to Newcastle ECS and is also added to the following night's up North Eastern TPO.

Midland Travelling Post Office Going North
Bristol (d 19.35), Gloucester, Birmingham (a 21.49, d 22.40), Derby (a 23.27, d 00.19), Sheffield, Doncaster, York (a 02.17, d 02.30),

Newcastle (a 04.06). Stock works north and south alternate nights.

Midland Travelling Post Office Going South

Newcastle (d 20.00), York (a 21.26, d 21.49), Sheffield, Derby (a 00.12, d 00.29), Birmingham (a 01.27, d 02.02), Gloucester, Bristol (a 04.28). Stock works north and south alternate nights.

North Eastern Travelling Post Office Night Down

London, King's Cross (d 22.30), Peterborough (a 23.32, d 23.48), York (a 01.41, d 01.53), Newcastle (a 02.28, d 03.30), Edinburgh (a 05.45). Except for one sorting carriage this TPO terminates at Newcastle and the stock forms part of the next night's up North Eastern TPO. The remaining sorting carriage continues to Edinburgh and becomes the next night's Edinburgh-York TPO.

North Eastern Travelling Post Office Night Up

Newcastle (d 20.54), York (a 22.24, d 22.34), Newark (a 23.16, d 23.31), Peterborough (a 01.07), d 01.19), London King's Cross (a 02.47). Stock forms the next night's London-York-Edinburgh TPO and the down North Eastern TPO. Passenger train throughout, Table 26.

North Western Travelling Post Office Night Down

London, Euston (d 22.50), Birmingham (a 00.29, d 00.47), Crewe (a 01.45, d 02.11), Preston (a 03.13, d 03.30), Carlisle (a 04.45). One sorting carriage is removed at Crewe and returned to London ECS to become part of the next night's North Western TPO; one stowage tender is removed at Preston and conveyed to Workington ECS for servicing; and one sorting carriage returns from Carlisle to Preston ECS to become part of the next night's Preston-London Bag Tender. The remainder of the stock continues to Glasgow ECS for servicing and becomes part of the Glasgow section of the Up Special TPO the next night.

Norwich-London Travelling Post Office

Norwich (d 18.45), Ipswich, London, Liverpool Street (a 21.04). Passenger train throughout, Table 11. Stock returns to

Norwich as the London-Norwich Bag Tender.

Peterborough-Crewe Travelling Post Office
Peterborough (d 20.25), Leicester, Derby (a 21.51, d 22.03), Crewe (a 23.16). Stock returns to Peterborough as the Crewe-Peterborough TPO. Lincoln section conveyed from Derby.

Peterborough-Crewe Travelling Post Office (Lincoln Section)
Lincoln (d 20.03), Newark, Nottingham, Derby (a 21.30). Added the Peterborough-Crewe TPO at Derby. Stock returns with the Crewe-Peterborough TPO.

Shrewsbury-York Travelling Post Office
Shrewsbury (d 22.50), Crewe (a 23.26, d 00.11), Stockport, Huddersfield, Leeds, York (a 02.50). Passenger train throughout, Tables

39, 87. Stock works east and west alternate nights.

South Wales Travelling Post Office Down
Bristol (d 01.24), Newport (a 01.53, d 02.05), Cardiff (a 02.26, d 02.48), Swansea, Carmarthen (a 05.06). Passenger train throughout, Tables 127, 128, 131. Stock returns to Swansea for servicing.

South Wales Travelling Post Office Up
Carmarthen (d 20.48), Swansea, Cardiff (a 22.42, d 23.00), Newport (a 23.14, d 23.29), Bristol (a 00.10). Passenger train throughout, Tables 127, 128, 131. Stock returns as the down service.

South Western Travelling Post Office Down
London, Waterloo (d 22.52), Southampton, Weymouth (a 03.32). Stock works up and down alternate nights.

South Western Travelling Post Office Up
Weymouth (d 22.38), Southampton, London, Waterloo (a 03.36). Stock works up and down alternate nights.

Below:
The Whitehaven-Huddersfield TPO leaving Millom on 6 May 1980. *C. Burnham*

Up Special Travelling Post Office

Aberdeen (d 15.47), Dundee, Perth (a 17.40, d 17.48), Motherwell, Carstairs, Carlisle (a 21.13, d 21.23), Preston (a 22.37, d 22.56), Crewe (a 23.50, d 00.22), Birmingham (a 01.25, d 01.52), London, Euston (a 03.58). Stock used to form the following night's Down Special TPO and North Western TPO. Passenger train from Dundee to Perth, Table 229.

Up Special Travelling Post Office (Edinburgh Section)

This service is known at TPO Section as the Edinburgh-Carstairs Bag Tender Duty. It operates using a BG and postal staff travel with it. A datestamp is carried for operational purposes and has been used on philatelic mail. At one time a basket was placed close to the van for late mail but this facility is no longer officially available.

Up Special Travelling Post Office (Glasgow Section)

Glasgow (d 19.30). Added to the Up Special TPO at Carstairs.

Whitehaven-Huddersfield Travelling Post Office

Whitehaven (d 18.50), Barrow-in-Furness, Preston (a 22.01, d 23.09), Manchester Victoria, Huddersfield (a 00.34). Train formation includes a stowage van en route from Workington to Preston for attaching to the Preston-London Bag Tender. Remaining stock returns as the Huddersfield-Whitehaven TPO.

York-Shrewsbury Travelling Post Office

York (d 22.34), Leeds, Huddersfield, Stockport, Crewe (a 00.11, d 02.25), Shrewsbury (a 03.02). Passenger train throughout, Tables 39, 87. Stock works east and west alternate nights.

Below:
Prior to making its cross-country journey to Shropshire, the York-Shrewsbury TPO stands at York on 5 April 1983. *Michael J. Collins*

5 A Personal Account of TPO Observations

The first travelling post office I ever saw was the Peterborough-Crewe. I posted some letters on it while it stood in Leicester station, waiting for the engine to run round and take it on its way to Crewe. The date was 29 August 1966; the service had been operating since 6 June that year. The rolling stock was of LMSR construction, now withdrawn.

The posting was made to add to a collection of postmarks associated with Leicester. It was not until 1971, when I joined the Railway Philatelic Group, that I learned more of the TPO network and was attracted by the postmarks and the names of the services. The latter were real relics of the past, many of them reflecting long defunct pre-grouping railway companies; the North Western night down, the Caledonian day up, the South Western, the Great Western, the North Eastern, the South Eastern, the Midland, the Highland. Then there were the Up Special and the Down Special — where could they run? What were their origins? What about the Manchester-Glasgow, the Carlisle-Edinburgh and the Crewe-Glasgow? These were not TPOs, they were sorting carriages, it said so on their postmarks. What did it mean? Was there any difference? There were others, too, and the whole lot obviously formed a cohesive group for forming a collection.

There are two ways of collecting current TPO postmarks. The easy way, using a specialist dealer, and the not so easy way, doing it yourself. (For obsolete material, of course, it is necessary to trade, either with dealers or with other collectors.)

I decided that more satisfaction was to be had if my collection was delivered individually by the postman. Starting in a small way with a visit to Derby in October 1971, I posted into both portions of the Peterborough-Crewe and the Midland in both directions. On returning to Leicester, by train, I did not have long to wait until the Crewe-Peterborough arrived to complete my first TPO expedition. I failed to note the details of all the rolling stock used but both sections of the Peterborough-Crewe had an LMSR sorting carriage. The Midland used two sorting vehicles, one LMSR and one LNER, in each direction.

My interest developed as I discovered more about the TPOs; that they operated as an interlocking network, not as a number of individual isolated services. For example, an urgent letter for London, too late for the last collection, could be helped on its way by posting it on the *northbound* Peterborough-Crewe at Leicester, leaving at 21.20. At Crewe it would be transferred to the southbound Up Special to arrive at Euston in time for the first delivery.

The nocturnal mailing expeditions continued, culminating in a postal marathon in October 1977. The use of a seven-day all-lines rail-rover ticket permitted visits to 11 centres and mailings on 22 TPOs. To date only four services remain unvisited.

When recounting details of some of these excursions to staff at TPO Section, when researching this volume, an unexpected response was forthcoming. It is one thing to see operations from the platform, but a better view would be obtained on on board. Would you like a trip?

Would I like a trip? Who would refuse such an offer? Not me. Yes please. Thank you. It was made clear that such offers were rarely made; it was essential that the routines were disturbed as little as possible as all the work is time critical. A convenient date and itinerary were arranged; the necessary permissions obtained and permits issued.

So it was that 20.00 on Thursday 9 February 1984 found me waiting at Leicester for the 18.45 High Speed Train from St Pancras which was bringing my travelling companions for the night. They were a representative from TPO Section and Simon Forty from Ian Allan Ltd. A visit was made to the 'Royal Mail' for fortifying refreshment and the objectives of the exercise were re-stated. The idea was to visit a small TPO, the Peterborough-Crewe to Crewe; a medium sized TPO, the Midland going south from Birmingham to Bristol; and a large TPO, the Up Special from Crewe to Birmingham. In this way it would be possible to gain an impression of how the TPO service works.

By 21.00 we were all on the platform at Leicester waiting for the TPO which duly arrived on time at 21.10. We boarded and introduced ourselves to the officer in charge, Roger Whitehead. While the bags of mail were being loaded and unloaded the locomotive, No 31 255, ran round the train. Departure

Above:
The crew of the Peterborough-Crewe TPO at Crewe on 9 February 1984. *Author*

Below:
One of the vehicles involved in the collision at Haughley Junction, No 80304 is shown here stabled at Stowmarket prior to being repaired. Apart from scratches and dents, there is a hole in the body under the 'Royal Mail' brand. 19 July 1982. *Michael J. Collins*

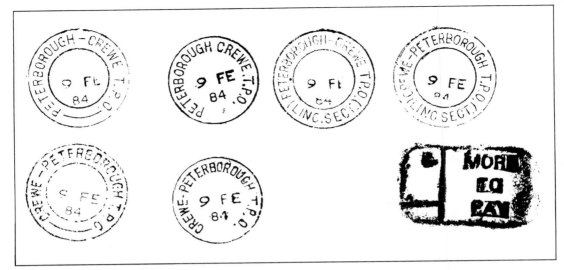

was on time, at 21.20, with a rake of four vehicles, one sorting, one stowage and two BGs — one at either end.

Once under way we signed the running sheet. This serves as a 'staff on duty' and time record for most TPOs. Roger Whitehead then gave us a conducted tour of the TPO. The stowage car was half used for stowage and half used for Datapost, with two sorters engaged on this duty. Four sorters were at the sorting frames, busy with the mail which had just come on board; late postings in Leicestershire and Northamptonshire destined for other TPOs and Ireland.

Being based at Peterborough the crews divide their time between the Crewe and East Anglian duties. Two members were on the latter when it was involved in a collision at Haughley Junction in 1982; sorting van E 80317 was turned on its side and Colin Flint suffered a broken collar bone. Until 1983 the men reckoned to work a five-year turn on the TPOs and were then relieved by their reserves. They are now able to undertake TPO duties for longer periods if they wish.

We were 8min late at Derby, being held at signals waiting for the platform to be cleared of a previous train. While the unloading and loading took place we hopped on to the platform to photograph the proceedings, keeping a weather eye open for the 'shunt'. In this move one of the BGs was left behind and the rest of the train was coupled on to the Lincoln portion of one sorting van and another BG.

Departure from Derby was 21min late and

a further 3min was to be lost before the next stop at Stoke-on-Trent. The mail being sorted now had been posted at Burton-on-Trent, Derby, Loughborough and Sheffield. The Peterborough men were aided by three Lincoln men; their sorting, of mails from Lincoln, Grantham, Newark and Nottingham having finished before Derby.

Now the train was complete I was able to complete a set of impressions of the datestamps and posted envelopes addressed to myself, suitably cancelled. I saw a missort, a letter posted at Melton Mowbray and addressed to London which should not have been on the TPO, backstamped to explain any delay. I can't help wondering about the reaction of the recipient had the significance of the backstamp been understood.

No further time was lost at Stoke and mails from that area were quickly taken on board. It was possible then for the crew to take a tea break, it being explained that this was the quieter of the two trips. The return working to Peterborough and Lincoln would have a large quantity of mails from other TPOs and Ireland for sorting; the labels on the sorting racks had already been changed. This was once a manual task, using chalk on a blackboard surface, but is now easily managed by using 'fillets'. These are PVC strips with the relevant names already painted on. They slide into slots under each row of pigeon holes. On some of the longer journeys the fillets could be changed several times en route.

Above left:
**Datestamp impressions from the Peterborough-
Crewe TPO and return.**

Above:
**Richard Escudier, 'Andy' Andreozzi and John
Harney on the Up Special TPO when the author
visited it on 9 February 1984.** *Author*

Crewe was reached 24min late but we still
had time in hand before the next stage of our
journey. The Peterborough-Crewe team had
agreed to pose for a photograph with their
sorting carriage, in the style of a number of
Victorian and Edwardian photographs which
still exist. They quickly gathered round after
completing the unloading and the photograph
was taken.

We walked across to the Up Special, noting
the Crewe-Cardiff and the Down Special as
we went. While we were at Crewe, the station
was also occupied by the Shrewsbury-York,
the York-Shrewsbury and the Preston-London
Bag Tender.

The Up Special, and its counterpart, the
Down Special, are probably the largest mail
trains with sorting operations in the world.
The Up Special runs with seven sorting vans,
five stowage vans and one BG. As we joined it
at Crewe there were 47 sorters, three
postmen and three supervisors. A further 15
sorters would join at Birmingham. The
maximum number of sorters on board at any
one time is about 70. The postmen stow the
made-up bags in the stowage vans.

We were introduced to the officer in
charge, 'Andy' Andreozzi, his assistant John
Harney and a Divisional Chief Inspector from
TPO Section, Richard Escudier. Since my trip,
Andy and John have retired.

John Harney commenced the tour by
showing us four of the five cars which formed
the Glasgow section. All five had left Euston
the previous day in the Down Special and had
reached Glasgow forming the Crewe-Glasgow
SC. On the day of our visit they had left
Glasgow as the Up Special (Glasgow Section),
joining the Up Special at Carstairs.

In order, the four cars were a stowage van
for Datapost; two sorting vans, one sorting for
Kent and Sussex (work which would be
mainly done by NW TPO men joining at
Birmingham), and one sorting for the Home
Counties; and a stowage van.

Richard Escudier was our guide for the rest
of the train. The fifth Glasgow car was sorting
mail for Hampshire, Dorset, East Anglia and
Essex. The next three cars had formed the
previous night's North Western Down, and in
addition to a stowage van, the sorting vans
were sorting for, respectively, London districts and London districts and foreign. The
final four cars had come from Aberdeen,
having been the Aberdeen portion of the
Down Special the previous day. Two sorting
vans were sorting for Berkshire, Wiltshire,
Buckinghamshire and Oxfordshire, and Staffordshire, Warwickshire and Worcestershire.
The two stowage vans are still known as the
Aberdeen Apparatus Brake and the Aberdeen
Letter Brake from former uses although the
apparatus has not been used since 1972.

The administrative centre of the train was
a table in the Glasgow stowage van. On
returning here the three supervisors started
reminiscing, 'Andy' Andreozzi, an ex-North
Eastern man, saying that the Great Western
had no idea about running mail trains.
Richard Escudier, a Western man, responded
by reminding him of a saying which once had
currency on the Western, 'the men of the
Western are the gentlemen of the TPOs'. They
told of a TPO staff magazine called *The
Traveller* which was full of gossip and news
of the TPOs and their staff. They talked of
using the apparatus, 'it was all right up to
about 80mph, but you kept well back when
those things [the pouches] came flying in'.
John Harney, started recounting some of the
tales which were passed on at the TPO school.

He produced the official TPO watch, resplendent in its leather pouch and told how, before the invention of wireless, this was the means of transmitting time throughout the country. Postmasters were instructed to synchronise their watches with the TPO watch, and because few could afford to own clocks in those days, this is the reason all Crown Post Offices have a clock in their windows. The officer in charge was supposed to synchronise the TPO watch with Big Ben before leaving London.

This conversation was accompanied by a continuous cry of 'mind your backs' as the postmen moved up and down the train with loaded mail bags. Before we knew it the train had arrived at Birmingham.

The southbound Midland TPO was waiting at the opposite face of the island platform as we pulled in to New Street. We crossed the platform and introduced ourselves to the officer in charge, David Bell. He had joined the train at Derby, having worked up from Bristol on the northbound duty. He and his 18-strong team accompanied a Newcastle crew, led by Colin Moore, as far as Birmingham. The Newcastle men would return home the following night.

Nine coaches made up the Midland TPO, one BG, four GUVs, and four Post Office cars. There were two sorting vans and two stowage vans. Sorting was being carried out for Gloucestershire, Somerset, Wiltshire, Bristol, Devon, Cornwall and Dorset. Extra work had come the way of this TPO since internal air mails from East Midlands Airport was being put on the train at Derby. It was noticeable that space was restricted in sorting van E80335 due to the room taken up by the now removed exchange apparatus. Half of one of the stowage vehicles was being used for Datapost. The use of steam heating made this train noticeably warmer than the electrically heated Up Special.

There are no pre-nationalisation vehicles in service now but the spirit of LMSR sorter No 30295 lives on in stowage van 80411, in the form of a large storage box/stool with the former's number on the side.

Each TPO duty has its own pouch. These are placed in the custody of the officers in charge and relate to the administration of the duty. David Bell opened his up and produced the records pertaining to his TPO. The sorting,

loading and circulation plans cover every aspect of mail handling, from the number of bags put on the train to the numbers put off when sorting has been completed.

The talk turned to shifts. Alan Turner told how the sorters worked three nights one week, followed by four nights the following week. David Bell worked Tuesday-Friday nights one week but the second week he would only work on Monday night; Wednesday-Friday of that week would be spent in the sorting office. Approaching Bristol the train had nearly completed its $8\frac{1}{2}$hr-journey from Newcastle but he still had to go into the sorting office before he could go home to Nailsea and bed.

Arrival at Bristol at 04.41, 13min late, ended the TPO tour and gave us over an hour to wait before we could catch the 06.00 to Paddington. We retreated to the Mail Office at the end of the platform where our host was an assistant inspector, responsible for overseeing the Post Office's operations at Temple Meads that night. Between midnight and 01.15, when he had the Great Western Up and Down, the South Wales and the Bristol-Derby in the station together, he had 110 men on the station, engaged in moving some 500 bags between the trains and the sorting office. There are 43 full time station postmen. Although the arrival of the southbound Midland TPO was nominally the last TPO business of the night to be dealt with, there was still the ghost of the Bristol-Plymouth to appease. The Bristol-Plymouth TPO was withdrawn in 1972; a passenger train runs in the same path and a postman-courier travels on it with Plymouth bound mails.

There was time to talk. An item of local(!) curiosity is the fact that mails from West Cornwall are routed on to the Great Western TPO at Penzance. They are taken off at Truro and flown to East Midlands Airport where they are transferred to Derby for forwarding by the Midlands TPO going north!

Christmas is a busy time for any Post Office. They well remember 1983 at Bristol as the year that a customer posted 5million items. It took $2\frac{1}{2}$ days and 31,000 bags to load them into 16 BGs. Talk of Christmas prompted talk of postal celebrations. During the run up to Christmas, when the TPOs are being run as bag tenders, the staff of the Great

Table

Timetable, with motive power and rolling stock used on the night of Thursday 9 February 1984.

Peterborough-Crewe TPO

		Schedule	Actual
Leicester (reverse)	a	21.10	21.10
	d	21.20	21.20
Derby (shunt and reverse)	a	21.51	21.59
	d	22.03	22.24
Stoke-on-Trent	a	22.48	23.12
	d	22.53	23.17
Crewe	a	23.16	23.40

Loco: Peterborough-Derby No 31255
Derby-Crewe No 31312
Stock: Peterborough section — M84098 (BG), E80408 (POT), E80350 (POS), M80901 (BG, removed at Derby). Lincoln section — E80306 (POS), M80848 (BG).

Up Special TPO

		Schedule	Actual
Crewe (attach BG)	d	00.22	00.25
Wolverhampton	a	00.59	01.11
	d	01.06	01.18
Birmingham (detach BG)	a	01.25	01.37

Despite a 12min late departure from Birmingham, 7min had been regained by Euston.

Loco: No 86244
Stock: Glasgow section (the previous night's Crewe-Glasgow SC) — M80418 (POT), M80393 (POS), M80377 (POS), M80419 (POT), M80376 (POS).
Glasgow section (the previous night's North Western TPO) — M80431 (POT), M80368 (POS), M80369 (POS).
Aberdeen section (the previous night's Down Special TPO) — M80341 (POS), M80375 (POS), M80424 (POT), M80456 (BPOT).
A BG from Manchester was conveyed to Birmingham.

Midland TPO Going South

		Schedule	Actual
Birmingham	a	02.02	02.09
Worcester	a	02.36	02.44
	d	02.51	02.59
Cheltenham	a	03.11	03.18
	d	03.21	03.28
Gloucester (reverse)	a	03.33	03.47
	d	03.46	03.58
Bristol (terminate)	a	04.28	04.41

Loco: No 45033
Stock: E93795 (GUV), M93262 (GUV), M80411 (POT), M80462 (POT), M80358 (POS), M80335 (POS), M80693 (BG), M93818 (GUV), M93169 (GUV).

BG — Gangwayed brake van
GUV — General utility van
POS — Post Office sorting van
POT — Post Office tender (stowage van)
BPOT — Brake Post Office tender

Western Down do one of their trips with a coach decorated, including fairy lights, and serving buffet refreshments. A highlight of these was the fresh strawberries! The day before Christmas a cornet player travels with them, playing carols at stations, a feat which attracts visitors to Temple Meads from miles around.

At the end the gossip always comes back to work. What happens if the trains are late? On the Up Special, for example, 20min late at Watford means that the first delivery is missed, negating the effort put in throughout the night. It became clear that the success of the postal operation depends upon a great deal of co-operation from all the parties involved.

At 05.30 we were able to get copies of the daily newspapers from the station kiosk, ready for boarding the 06.00 High Speed Train back to Paddington. The toasted bacon sandwiches I had on the train were the best I've ever tasted.

On this note we ended our tour of the TPO service. In one night it was not possible to gain a great insight into the operations but it was a truly fascinating experience. I was left with an overwhelming impression of friendly staff trying very hard to maintain a service in a situation they could not totally control. I shall never forget the large amounts of mail being sorted at speed, especially on the Up Special, where there appeared to be as many full bags in the sorting cars as in the stowage vans.

Appendix – TPO Postmarks and Philatelic Material

1890.

The study of postmarks, and other instructional or informative markings applied to posted items, probably followed closely behind the interest taken in stamps shortly after the 1d black was introduced in 1840. Certainly by the time J. G. Hendy wrote his monumental *History of the Travelling Post Offices compiled from official records* in 1905 he thought enough of this aspect to include detailed information on the various types of markings used on the early services. He was well placed to do this, being the curator of the General Post Office's Record Room.

The Post Office Archive is probably the largest single source of information for anyone interested in the TPOs. In addition to the usual business records it contains the Impression Books. Their pages bear impressions of nearly every postal marking ever issued. Unfortunately there are gaps in the collection but many TPO strikes are recorded, some being otherwise unknown.

The other major source of information relating to TPO postmarks lies in items which have passed through the postal system and subsequently come into the hands of

collectors. Fortunately most collectors are gregarious in nature and readily share the information at their disposal.

The use of postmarks to show the origins of a postal item originated in London in 1661 and gradually spread until their usage was common throughout the country. The first travelling post offices were not issued with datestamps because it was not intended that they should receive loose mail from the public. There was a need, however, to show why a letter was delayed through missorting, ie being sent to a TPO in error. Therefore the first markings associated with TPOs were not concerned with the place of posting but were to provide information.

The experimental TPO of 1838 was issued with a stamp which read, 'Missent to London & Birmingham Railway'. Less informative stamps containing initials, such as 'EGW' (evening, Great Western) or 'IRPOM' (Irish, Railway Post Office, morning), served the same purpose. The earliest types contained their message in straight lines without

Right:
Nine different Tax marks used on TPOs. They were used on: a) the East Anglian TPO (down) in 1972; b) the East Anglian TPO (up) in 1972; c) the Highland TPO in 1976; d) the Midland TPO in 1976; e) the Caledonian TPO in 1978 — this one was held together with string; f) the Huddersfield-Whitehaven TPO in 1972; g) the Peterborough-Crewe TPO in 1971; h) the South Wales TPO in 1973; i) the Highland TPO in 1977 — this type should now be used on all TPOs.

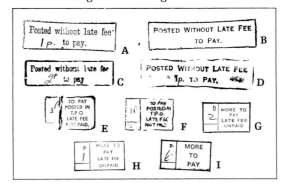

borders; later ones were shaped as stars, lozenges or circles.

The first circular datestamps were issued in the late 1860s/early 1870s. With few exceptions the name of the TPO was placed around the edge, within a border. The date was placed in the centre of the stamp, usually in two straight lines. They were mostly $\frac{13}{16}$in or $\frac{15}{16}$in diameter. The space above the date was often used to show the time or, by using letters or numerals, to show operational data. This could be an indication to show if the datestamp was being used on a day or a night mail, or an up or a down duty, or to show which crew was using it. A few of the smaller sorting carriages were issued with circular stamps which had no dates. In these instances the name of the service was placed across the centre.

The public were allowed, subject to payment of a late fee, to post letters on the TPOs from 1860. Items posted without the late fee were held back and forwarded by the normal service. In 1891 it was decided to accept such items, with a surcharge of double the deficiency being levied on the recipient.

Below:
A registered envelope posted on the Up Special TPO.

Boxed rectangular surcharge marks reading 'Posted without late fee 1d to pay' on two lines were issued. These tended to vary in size but the usual dimensions were about $2\frac{1}{2}$in by $\frac{5}{8}$in.

A new type of datestamp was introduced from the 1890s. The outer diameter was 1in, the layout as before but the name was separated from the date by an inner ring, $\frac{5}{8}$in in diameter. For services with a short name the space was filled with one or two thick arcs at the base. Collectors know these as 'double ring datestamps with thick arcs'.

This issue was replaced from the 1950s by similar stamps having thin arcs where necessary.

At the same time the introduction of a new type of tax mark commenced. These measured $1\frac{1}{8}$in by $\frac{3}{4}$in and read '1d to pay posted in TPO late fee not paid'. Each TPO had its own issue showing its PO number, a feature of some of the older types. In 1970 the surcharge marks were replaced again. The new issue was the same size but read '—d more to pay late fee unpaid', allowing the amount due to be inserted by hand. The PO number was not shown, allowing bulk production. They had a short life, being replaced, after decimalisation in 1971, by an issue which indicated the new currency.

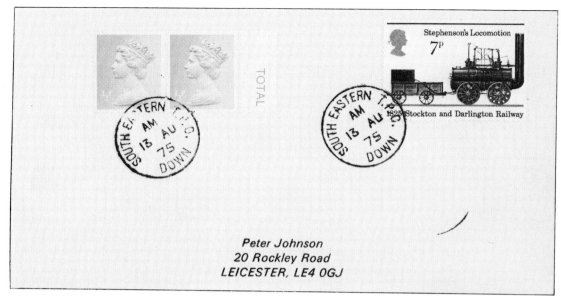

Peter Johnson
20 Rockley Road
LEICESTER, LE4 0GJ

Since 1970 many services have been issued with single-ring datestamps. These are for use on documents relating to the Datapost service and should not be used to cancel stamps, although such use sometimes does occur.

In March 1977, following the abolition of the late fee the previous September, the TPOs were issued with a tax stamp which read simply '—p more to pay'. This is for use on

Above:
Single ring AM datestamp impressions.

Below:
A cover showing thin arc and thick arc double ring postmarks.

Right:
The Uniform Penny Postage jubilee envelope.

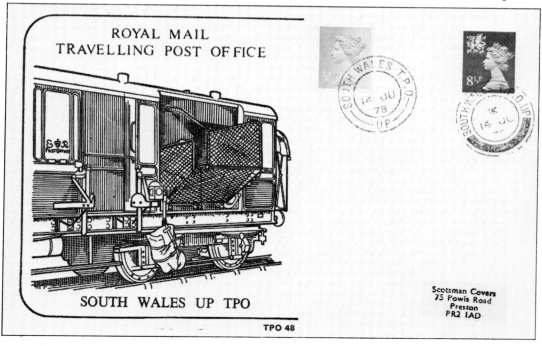

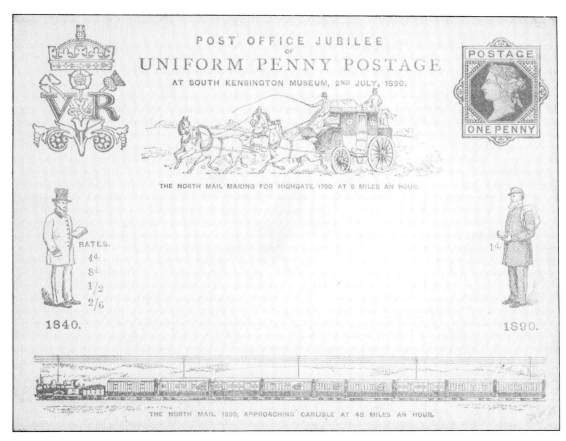

underpaid mail and is the same size as previous issues.

Two further matters relating to the datestamps are worthy of comment. The first is that although many services run throughout the night the date is not changed at midnight for administrative reasons. As a result an interesting situation was created for collectors when new stamps were issued. It was possible to buy the new issues at midnight at the 24hr post office in London's Trafalgar Square. The stamps were affixed to first day covers and posted on to Up TPOs which arrived at London sufficiently late for those collectors who hurried to reach them at the penultimate station on their route. The result was a first day cover dated the day before the stamps were issued. In 1953 the GPO took steps to eliminate this anomaly. On the nights when new stamps were issued the TPOs concerned were issued with a reserve datestamp bearing the correct date but with the letters AM above it; this was to allow a distinction to be made with the following night's mail which would be cancelled with the same date. The outcome was an even more collectable item for collectors! The development of the motorway system allowed trains to be reached at even greater distances. AM postmarks could be obtained on the North Western Down and the Huddersfield-Whitehaven TPOs by travelling to Preston and getting there before 03.30! All this came to an end when the Tragalgar Square office ceased to open all night in 1981. In 1963 the Forth Road Bridge stamps were placed on sale at midnight in Edinburgh, creating new opportunities for just one occasion.

The second matter for comment relates to side numbers. On the longer trips a crew will make a down journey the first night and return with the up on the second night. A second crew will be working in the opposite direction. To distinguish them the first will be called side 1, the second side 2. These distinctions are shown on the datestamps, so it is possible to post on the same train two nights running and get different postmarks. There are some variations to this — the Huddersfield-Whitehaven is side 1, the Whitehaven-Huddersfield is side 2, yet this is an out and back trip worked by the same crew. Edinburgh based crews take over the London-York-Edinburgh and North Eastern Down TPOs at Newcastle using datestamps without side numbers, but with the letter E above the date. On the North Western and the South Western TPOs it is possible to get different postmarks at different ends of the trains.

There is a considerable knack to the art of striking good datestamp impressions on *terra firma*, so it can be imagined that attempting this undertaking on a moving train is somewhat hazardous. Hand in any philatelic mail as early as possible so that the crew stands a reasonable chance of cancelling the stamps before departure.

The Post Office has issued a few commemorative items associated with TPOs and the carriage of mail by rail over the years. The number is very small; a stamp, some postal stationery and a few postmarks.

In chronological order the first item to be issued saw the light of day on 2 July 1890. It was an envelope issued to commemorate the jubilee of universal penny postage. In addition to an impressed 1d stamp, the envelope bears some illustrative motifs. There are comparative illustrations of postmen of 1840 and 1890, with the rates of postage applicable to their times, 4d to 2/6d and 1d. A horse-drawn north mail making for Highgate at 8mph in 1790 is contrasted with the rail equivalent making for Carlisle at 48mph in 1980. The latter is hauled by an LNWR 2-2-2 and consists of nine coaches, including four sorting carriages with apparatus nets. One of the mail coaches is a six-wheeler, the rest of the train being bogie stock, so it is reasonable to assume that it is an accurate representation of the typical train of the period. The envelope and correspondence card, enclosed, sold for 1/- at an exhibition held at South Kensington.

On 4 October 1962 the Postal History Society issued a postcard for its 18th annual conference held at King's Lynn. The address side is impressed with a 3d stamp and carried a suitable text. The reverse is illustrated with a sketch of the first train carrying mail across the River Ouse when the East Anglian Railway was opened to King's Lynn on 25 October 1847. A tracing of a datestamp impression of the King's Lynn section of the East Anglian TPO Up is also shown.

Below:

A commemorative cover posted on the North Western TPO on the last night of apparatus working. The event took place after midnight but the TPO datestamp wasn't changed.

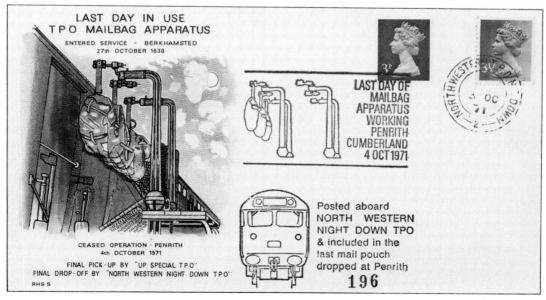

The 51st Philatelic Congress of Great Britain was held in Bristol in 1969. A series of one-day postmarks illustrating different aspects of the congress was sponsored. That for GPO Day, 26 June, illustrates a six-wheeled mail coach which purports to be GWR No 1.

Another postcard was issued, by the Railway Philatelic Group, in conjunction with its annual convention held at Doncaster on 10 October 1970. A 4d stamp was impressed on the address side, while the reverse stamp was illustrated with a drawing of Stirling's single, No 1, then commemorating its centenary, supported by relevant TPO datestamp impressions.

The Post Office itself sponsored a special one day postmark which was used at Penrith on 4 October 1972. The occasion was the last use of the mailbag exchange apparatus. The postmark shows loaded and empty lineside standards.

On 26 November 1979 the South Western Postal Region celebrated the 150th anniversary of Swindon post office. The card, entitled 'Mail trains of the South West' is notable because none of the four trains illustrated is a mail train! They all have connections with the Great Western Railway or the Western Region; an 'Iron Duke' class broad gauge locomotive of 1891, 'King' class *King George V* on railtour duty, diesel-hydraulic D1013 *Western Ranger*, and a high speed train. A 'jumbo' version of the same card was issued on 12 March 1980, to coincide with the issue of the Liverpool & Manchester Railway Stamps. It was this set which included a stamp featuring a mail coach. Five stamps were issued in a strip, showing *Rocket* and typical coaches of the period; the resultant train couldn't be more atypical! On the same day the stamp were issued the post offices of Liverpool and Manchester commenced franking ordinary mail with slogan postmarks which read 'Liverpool to Manchester 150 years of mail by rail Collect Post Office commemorative covers — ring Freefone 6666'. The motif was a four-wheel sorting carriage complete with exchange apparatus, so obviously not of 1830 vintage.

The station at Crewe is the centre of TPO operations so it was logical for the Post Office to arrange a TPO exhibition there. A display was arranged in a sorting carriage and a commemorative cover and postmark were issued to coincide with the stamps.

Also on 12 March 1980 the North West Postal Board reissued a postcard it had first issued on 11 November 1976. It illustrated Ackermann's print of Liverpool & Manchester Railway passenger trains, one of them including a mail coach.

The Romford & Upminster Railway Users Association used the issue as an excuse to sponsor a special postmark which cancelled the stamps on first day covers posted at Emerson Park, the only intermediate station on the line. It was inscribed 'Havering's own railway celebrates 150 years mail on rail'.

Many of the Post Office coaches in use today were built at Wolverton works, so when the works' open day was held, on 16 August 1980, a special postmark featured the link by illustrating a representation of one of the early sorting carriages.

The 150th anniversary of the carriage of mail by rail was commemorated with a special postmark on 11 November 1980. It was used at Manchester and featured Liverpool's Moorish Arch.

On 1 October 1981 the Post Office became a public corporation and marked the event by publishing a set of six postcards illustrating its transport operations. One of the cards showed the down Great Western TPO at Paddington.

The Midlands Postal Board issued a set of two postcards featuring the Shrewsbury-York TPO on 2 November 1981. One shows the TPO being loaded at Shrewsbury, the other, the interior. Arrangements were made for collectors to have cards posted on the train, and on the York-Shrewsbury TPO, so that they could have the service datestamps applied. Special postmarks were also available for both duties, but postcards thus cancelled were not carried on the train.

The external view of the Shrewsbury-York TPO was also used on a card, issued by the London Postal Region in September 1982, featuring mail handling at Paddington. The multi-view card also showed the Post Office's underground railway, the vehicular loading dock and the exterior of the station.

On a number of occasions from 4 June 1984, a postmark inscribed 'The World's Smallest TPO' was applied to mail posted at

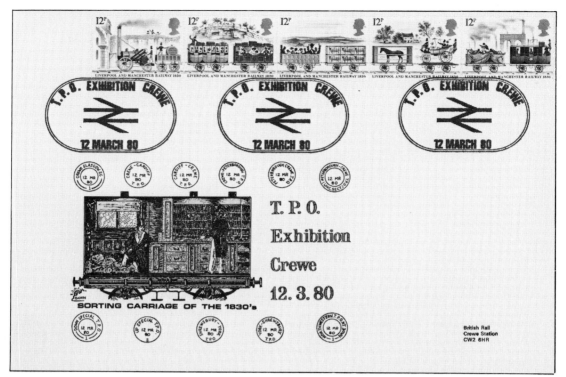

Above:
The Liverpool & Manchester Railway anniversary stamps featured the L&M postal van. They are seen on a first day cover posted at the Crewe TPO exhibition.

Below:
The L&M postmark slogan featuring a sorting carriage.

Below right:
The special cover produced for the 30th anniversary of the Derby-Bristol TPO.

the International Garden Festival, held in Liverpool from 2 May-14 October that year. A 15in gauge railway was constructed to carry visitors around the site, and whilst the railway did carry mail on the dates the postmark was used, the TPO designation was incorrect as it was not sorted on the train. The Post Office issued a postcard of the railway with the same designation.

In addition to these official issues a number of private issues have been made from time to

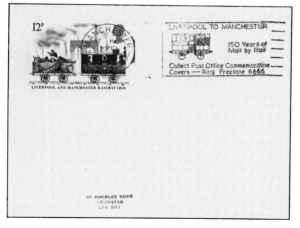

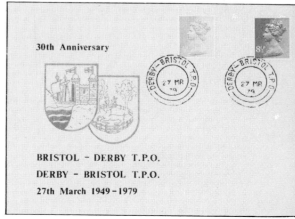

time. A few of them are worthy of comment. They usually take the form of specially produced covers posted on TPOs to coincide with, or commemorate, a particular event.

The TPO centenary was the occasion for a cover which was posted on the Birmingham-Crewe TPO on 6 January 1938. This was the anniversary of the experimental TPO which ran on the Grand Junction Railway. A similar cover was posted on the same TPO on 17 September 1938 to mark the creation of the first permanent TPO on the London & Birmingham Railway 100 years earlier.

From 1977 to 1980 Scotsman Cover Services produced a series of covers posted on TPOs. The aim was to obtain datestamp impressions from every TPO, including all possible variations. Except for the name of the TPO concerned a standard cover design was used. Over 100 varieties were available when the exercise was completed. Mailings included the last runs of the Crewe-Bangor TPO, the South Eastern TPO and the Manchester-Glasgow SC.

On 2 March 1979 the 50th anniversary of the East Anglian TPO was commemorated with a special cover posted on the train. The cover was illustrated with the shields of London and Norwich. The shields of Bristol and Derby illustrated a similar cover which marked the 30th anniversary of the Bristol-Derby TPO on 27 March 1979.

The 814 Group, custodians of GWR TPO 814 at Didcot, have published three postcards

of their vehicle, to raise funds, since 1981. Many of these have been put through the exchange apparatus at Didcot and then posted on the Great Western TPO.

No mention has been made concerning the value of the items mentioned in this section. Undoubtedly some are very rare, while some will be equally common. As with many things prices are usually governed by supply and demand; there are still bargains to be had.

Above:
The reverse of a postcard posted on the Great Western Railway TPO at Didcot. After being put through the exchange apparatus it was posted on the Great Western TPO. The labels are sold to raise funds for No 814; one is affixed to every item put through the exchange.

Below:
A cover carried on the LNER TPO at the Great Central Railway on the occasion of its first public demonstration.

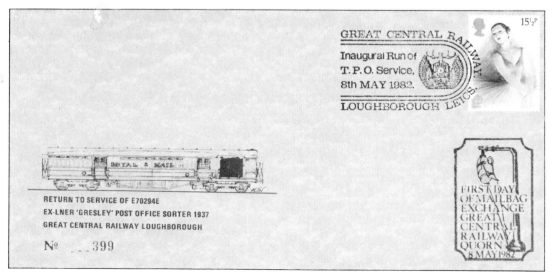

A Selected Bibliography

Philatelic

Goodbody, A. M.; *An Introduction and Guide to the Travelling Post Offices of Great Britain*; Railway Philatelic Group, 2nd Edition 1983.

Haram, V. S.; *Centenary of the Irish Mail 1848-1948*; Railway Executive, London Midland Region, 1948.

Harvey, A. M.; *Travelling Post Offices, Bag Tenders Etc of Great Britain and Ireland from 1838*; unpublished manuscript, 1960.

Hendy, J. G.; *History of the Travelling Post Offices compiled from official records*; unpublished manuscript, 1905.

Hendy, J. G.; *History of the Mail Bag Exchange Apparatus compiled from official records*; unpublished manuscript, 1905.

Hill, Norman; *TPO Postmarks of the British Isles*; Author, 1962.

Hill, Norman; *The Railway Travelling Post Offices of Great Britain and Ireland 1838-1975*; Harry Hayes, 1977.

Hosegood, J. G.; *Great Western Railway Travelling Post Offices*; Wild Swan Publications Ltd, 1983.

Obradovic, A.; *The TPO Network; notes for a lecture;* presented to the Chartered Institute of Transport (Western Section), 1984.

Rowden, J. J. C.; *The Travelling Post Office*; General Post Office (Green Paper No 24), 1936.

Ward, C. W.; *English TPOs — Their History and Postmarks;* Author 1949.

Ward, C. W.; *Irish TPOs — Their History and Postmarks*; Author, 1938.

Ward, C. W.; *Scottish TPOs — Their History and Postmarks*; Author, 1947.

Wilson, H. S.; *TPO A History of the Travelling Post Offices of Great Britain Part 1 England — The Specials and Associated TPOs*; Railway Philatelic Group, 3rd Edition 1979.

Wilson, H. S.; *TPO A History of the Travelling Post Offices of Great Britain Part 2 England — South of the Midland TPO*; Railway Philatelic Group, 2nd Edition, 1979.

Wilson, H. S.; *TPO A History of the Travelling Post Offices of Great Britain Part 3 Scotland and Ireland*; Railway Philatelic Group, 1977.

Rolling Stock

Casserley, R. M. & Millard, P. A.; *A Register of West Coast Joint Stock*; Historical Model Railway Society, 1980.

Ellis, C. H.; *Railway Carriages in the British Isles 1830-1914*; Allen & Unwin, 1965.

Essery, R. J. & Jenkinson, D.; *The LMS Coach*; Ian Allan, 1969.

Gould, D.; *Carriage Stock of the SECR*; Oakwood, 1976.

Gould, D.; *Maunsell's SR Steam Passenger Stock 1923-1939*; Oakwood, 1978.

Harris, M.; *Great Western Coaches 1890-1954*; David & Charles, 1966.

Harris, M.; *Gresley's Coaches*; David & Charles, 1973.

Harris, M.; *Preserved Railway Coaches*; Ian Allan, 1976.

Hunter, D. L. G.; *Carriages & Waggons of the Highland Railway*; Turntable Enterprises, 1971.

Kidner, R. W.; *Service stock of the Southern Railway*; Oakwood, 1980.

Larkin, D.; *BR General Parcels Rolling Stock — A pictorial survey;* D. Bradford Barton, 1978.

Mountford, E. R.; *A Register of GWR Absorbed Stock*; Oakwood, 1978.

Newbury, P. J.; *Carriage Stock of the London, Brighton & South Coast Railway*; Oakwood, 1975.

Parkin, K.; *Locomotive Hauled Mark 1 Coaching Stock of British Railways;*; Historical Model Railway Society, 1983.

Further reference will be found in George Ottley's *Bibliography of Railway History*; HMSO 2nd Edition 1983, and Supplement 1984.